THE WORLD IN MY HEART

a personal exploration
of
spirituality and awareness

Jo Farrow

QUAKER HOME SERVICE
LONDON

First published May 1990
by Quaker Home Service
Friends House, Euston Road, London NW1 2BJ

F13

Cover design by John Blamires
based on a painting by Jo Farrow

Printed in Great Britain in Palatino 11/12
by Headley Brothers Ltd, Invicta Press,
Ashford, Kent and London

Contents

1   Turning Point   page   1

2   Year of Jubilee   14

3   Knowing Experimentally   24

4   In and Out of Time   32

5   My Own Woman   42

6   Moments of Awareness   52

7   Heart Work   61

8   Spirituality as Awareness   74

9   The Waste Land   88

10   Waiting in the Dark   104

11   Silence, Simplicity and Integration   113

    References   124

Acknowledgements

This is not the book I intended or even wanted to write. When I began it I was aware of a sharp dispute between the different members of my 'committee of selves'. Some wanted it to be clever, discursive and giving nothing away. My Puritan self wanted to conceal the more disreputable bits. Another part of me, resisted by all the rest, was willing to be a fool, perhaps a holy one, and give myself away.

Many Friends supported the holy fool and gave practical help and good counsel when I began to write the book. I cannot name them all, but thanks must go to colleagues in Friends House for giving me freedom from other commitments in order to write it, to the Literature Committee for encouraging me to begin, and complete it; to Beth Allen for taking over my workload, to Elizabeth Cave for wise editorial assistance and enthusiastic support, to Clifford Barnard for coming back from well-earned retirement to see it through to finished production and to Jim Pym and David Goddard for assisting him; to Angela Brew for helping me to say 'yes' to the holy fool and to the wise woman, to my mother, who prays without ceasing, and to Joan, who is a root of my hope.

JO FARROW

The pearl is hid in the field, and the field in the world and the world is in your hearts, and there you must dig deep to find it, and when you have digged deep and found it, you must sell all to purchase and redeem this field.[1]

George Fox.

My heart is touched by all I cannot save
So much has been destroyed.

I have to cast my lot with those,
who age after age, perversely.

With no extraordinary power
Re-constitute the world.[2]

Adrienne Rich, 'Natural Resources' in
Dream of a Common Language.

Each mortal thing does one thing and the
    same;
Deals out that being indoors each one dwells:
Selves—goes itself, myself it speaks and
    spells
Crying what I do is me: for this I came.[3]

Gerard Manley Hopkins, Selected Poems.

Chapter 1
Turning Point

'There still exists a long, long way to go before
spirituality as living and sharing life replaces
the sentimental and oppressive spiritualities of
idealism and other-worldliness.'[1]

Matthew Fox, *On Becoming a Musical, Mystical
Bear.*

'Being committed to God is not about being
nice. It is about being real.'[2]

Esther de Waal, *Living with Contradiction.*

'Prayer is the language by which we as human
beings offer and assert our own selves. It is the
language by which we are totally open to who
we are and with which we offer who we are to
who it is that God is. It is, as it were, the basic
language of honesty about ourselves.'[3]

Melvyn Matthews, *The Hidden Journey.*

This book was written at a turning point in my life. In a few
months from its publication I shall be a senior citizen,
taking my first steps into the unfamiliar territory of retirement. Inevitably I have found myself looking back at all the
roads that have brought me to this new point of arrival and
departure. So much of our life is punctuated by moments
like this, so many deaths and entrances, so many experiences of letting go, and moving into the new.

I have written about the things I have discovered en
route, the things I 'know experimentally'. Sometimes I
have been surprised at how much I knew in the hidden
places of my life and also how hard I found it to trust that
inward knowing. When I look back I can see now how
many things I tried to carry in my rucksack that did not
belong to my experience as a woman. I hope that what I
have struggled to tell will be of some encouragement to

1

others who, like me, have found it hard to cherish and love the world in their own hearts, or to trust their own wisdom and spiritual insights. Becoming a Friend has helped me to dig deeper and unearth the treasure, but there were hints and glimpses of it long before I came to value the profound insights of Quaker spirituality.

What I have written is from the perspective of a latecomer to the Society of Friends. I have spent forty years deeply involved in the life of another nonconformist church, twenty-six of them as a Methodist Deaconess and eleven of those working as a teacher of art and language in a school for children with special learning difficulties. For the first decade of my life I had no formal contact with any church.

Peculiar paradoxes are part of my inheritance. Nonconformity is somehow in my blood and bones, a legacy from Huguenot ancestors and a Scandinavian great-grandmother. Dissidence and heresy come more naturally to me than orthodoxy. Yet my understanding and misunderstanding of Christian spirituality owe far more to models of holy living developed in the Orthodox and Anglo-Catholic tradition. I have been helped and hindered by them for most of my life.

And from the beginning of my exposure to monastic and noncomformist images of holiness and the more conventional models of Christian living I have been aware, intermittently, of a different way of knowing God, as intimate and direct as a child's perception of reality. I have glimpsed it in the fertile sub-soil of the mystical tradition in all religions, and found it hidden in the depths of my own being. It is like the hidden streams of fresh water which nourish the long swathes of downland in the part of Sussex to which I belong.

What I have written is addressed to Friends, though I know that others will read it. I have tried to avoid as much as possible the peculiar household vocabulary that is dear to many Friends and to re-interpret it for myself and others in ways that belong more to our contemporary awareness. But it has been within the Quaker discipline of waiting on God in the silence of the heart that I have learned to be more friendly to my inner world and accept the inconsistencies and contradictions that have come to light in the exercise.

Some of the gentleness towards myself, which is still new to me, I have learned from insights and exercises gleaned from the human potential movement. For some years they took me further in self-knowing than the more traditional disciplines of Christian mysticism which have the same end. I have come back to some of those enriched by the experience of learning from the self-awareness exercises of humanistic psychology.

This book is an attempt to integrate all that has been important to me in the Biblical tradition and Christian story with all that I have learned about my own story from the women's movement, feminist theology and the insights of depth psychology. Each has enriched the others, unlocked the doors of perception for me and helped me to move between them and come home to myself.

*   *   *

My awareness of living at a crucial turning point in my own journey coincides with what many perceive as a turning point in Western society. We seem to be living, awkwardly, hopefully and sometimes painfully between the ending of one age and the birth contractions of another. It may well be a moment of crisis and evolution as great as that which preceded the renaissance and the age of enlightenment. It is not the books I read which confirm my own sense of living on the edge of a new age. I know it at a much deeper place in my life.

The real questions that have tantalised me as I wrote this book have very little to do with whether I am a Quaker universalist, a new age woman or simply an old-fashioned Jesus freak. (He was the front-runner of the new age and as contemporary as God is.) They have much more to do with what kind of primal therapy may be required to re-birth or re-condition us for a new experiment in holistic living. Unless we can learn how to squeeze through the narrow gateway into the new age and live together without defences this may well be the last turning point in human history.

Friends have some of the insights that are needed. Others are lodged in more unexpected places. We are often strangely reluctant to talk about the treasures of our tradition. Doing the truth or befriending it has had a higher priority for us than theorising about it. Talking about God has seemed less important than listening to the spirit and walking in the light. We may have to overcome our reticence and find fresh ways of telling what we know. God talk is often, but not always, cheaper than God work.

In spite of our reticence about credal affirmations and God language we seem to be having a fresh outburst of problems to do with religious experience and Christian language. We find it difficult to say anything at all without hiccoughs or bringing some Friends out in allergic spots. We keep upsetting one another because some of us are temperamentally disposed to wordless and image-free communication with a deep mysterious something or other. (What Rudolph Otto called the *mysterium tremendum*.)[4] Whilst others of us are quite at home praying to a Jesus whose human face seems to tell us all that we need to know about the mystery. Some of us are into the Cosmic Christ or the Christ who is the archetype for the human journey of self-knowing and God-becoming. And some of us manage to play among all the metaphors without actually rupturing our spiritual spleens.

All of us, I suspect, know far more than we realise; but find it hard to articulate what we have discovered of God in our deepest human experiences. The most pervasive models of spirituality developed in the Western church have conditioned us to devalue or distrust those experiences and it is hard to decontaminate our perception and rediscover what we know in the depths of our experience.

Some of our traditional ways of 'picturing' God are unhelpful to us when it comes to solving the huge problems of our time. Some of our more conventional images of holiness are more inhibiting than helpful to us in creating a global theology and a spirituality which is inclusive rather than elitist and deeply exclusive. But I do not think, as some do, that it is God who needs updating.

*   *   *

I have met a number of Friends who talk with great excitement about new age thinking. They manage to sound rather sophisticated about it all in spite of the fact that the 'all' appears to include a very strange mixture of primitive and medieval stuff like tarot cards, astrology and shamanism. It seems a fascinating but bewildering concoction of Jungian psychology, new physics, medieval alchemy and earth goddesses, liberally laced with holistic medicine and Green politics. The fact that I am a bit 'flip' about it shows that I am not into it yet. It may be a sign of the wisdom of old age or my natural irreverence popping up again. Discernment is, however, a gift of the spirit, and we need a lot of that too if we are going to find our way through the Age of Aquarius without drowning in it.

The truth is that I do not belong in either world. I am awkwardly astride a growing credibility gap. The old religious language and imagery sometimes reflects but often contradicts my own experience. The patriarchal bias of the Biblical tradition, the structures of church life and conventional piety are difficult areas for me now. They reflect a view of the world that is not mine. They have played some part in making it much harder for me to trust my own experiences as a woman. They express the faith of those who lived in a different age. I salute their courage and integrity in living the truth as they saw it but I cannot walk in their shoes.

But I am not yet a paid up member of the new age. I am aware of moral rigidities, puritan prejudices and strong individualistic tendencies which seem to disqualify me even if I wanted to apply for full membership.

We do not know yet what patterns of religious life or community will emerge from this breaking up of the old or what kinds of spirituality will emerge from this time of transition. We do not know whether we shall find a common language to speak of the things that matter most to us or whether all that is requried of us is the grace and humour to

5

celebrate our differences. It may be that we shall find our unity in other ways, perhaps simply as 'birthright members of the human race' as David Robson suggested in our 1989 Yearly Meeting session on 'Justice, Peace and the Integrity of Creation'. It may be that he was right in saying that the problems which confront the human race today are so huge that all our religious labels and sectarian stances are totally irrelevant. And it may be that only in the kind of worship that Quakers in London Yearly Meeting have held in trust for over three hundred years shall we find a unity in naked intent before God that goes beyond the words that are so problematic for us.

*   *   *

Even the word 'spirituality' has an awkwardness about it in spite of its fashionable new look. It is too abstract and vague. What does it mean for us now in the age of liberation movements and Green politics? For some of us it reeks of medieval dualisms and other-worldliness. I find it surprising that in a time of the burgeoning of movements concerned with more holistic approaches it should still be in vogue. But it is. Perhaps it goes hand-in-hand with our fascination with higher consciousness, neo-gnosticism and dabbling in the occult.

I have about as much higher consciousness as our two cats, (rather less in their estimation) and I walk with two feet on an earth too teeming with miracles to crave for anything more extraordinary. But my real reticence is not simply a preference for an earthy and earth-loving awareness. It is also a reluctance to go in for too much classy or exclusive stuff. Being a Quaker is a bit élitist but I chose it because there has always been a sturdy, down-to-earth quality about Quaker spirituality. Its agenda is not the cultivation of private spiritual allotments or even higher consciousness. In spite of regressions and failure we have stubbornly refused to separate prayer and pragmatics, mysticism and mending the world. We have moved between the cloister and the market place and tried to live

6

the awkward questions between them without loosing our balance too often.

I suppose I am uneasy myself about the word 'spirituality' because it is redolent with hierarchical assumptions about reality, setting against one another, or ranking in order, things which seem to belong together in holy equality. We separate them at our peril—body and spirit, sacred and secular, women and men, reason and emotion, this world and the next. It has taken me years to come to the point of recognising how deeply those dualisms have conditioned and infected my own consciousness.

*   *   *

In spite of its awkwardness, I find that I need to reclaim the word spirituality and fill it out again with the meaning it has for me if I remember that the word used for 'spirit' in the New Testament meant, literally, 'breath'. It was used to describe the difference between being only half alive and fully alive, between being aware of the purpose of life and missing it completely.

Badly translated and soaked in the dualisms of platonic thought it has often been used to define a way of being religious rather than a way of being in touch with the deepest sources of life within ourselves. It has been distorted to justify withdrawing from life rather than going further into it, and to draw artificial boundaries between some supposedly more élite part of ourselves and all that makes us real human beings capable of making a spirited response to life.

I may not like the way in which the word 'spirit' has been mutilated but I can at least wrestle with it and compel it to yield up its real meaning for me. I do not like what Quakers have sometimes done with it. We have our own brand of dualism. In spite of our continual affirmation that the whole of life is sacramental, we have practiced our own version of 'splitting off' and have sometimes talked as if 'worship in spirit and in truth' was about putting down our minds and bodies and saying a very firm 'cool it' to our emotions.

When I wrestle with what those words from John's Gospel mean for me I believe they are much more to do with bringing the whole of myself into the difficult exercise of being honest to God and therefore to others and to myself. 'In spirit' means from the deepest part of my life where all that I am is strangely linked with all that God is. Our Quaker vocabulary about 'being centred' is all about reaching individually and together that dynamic point of contact. 'In truth' means reaching that same depth and allowing the searching light of the spirit to show me the self-deceptions and humbug with which I hide from reality. Prayer is after all not a matter of being nice or respectable but about shedding our illusions and being real before God.

In this book I have tried to reclaim the word spirituality as shorthand for the long process of becoming aware of reality, its darkest as well as its brightest and loveliest aspects. I want to reclaim it because I believe we are moving into an age when prayer and spirituality must be about our awareness of the whole of life and our radical response to it. We are no longer, as David Robson reminded us at Aberdeen Yearly Meeting, like Bunyan's pilgrim, with his sense of impending disaster, travelling away from the city of destruction to save our own souls. Any view of salvation as a purely individual affair will not do for us now. Our planet is potentially one huge disaster zone and we cannot enjoy the luxury of private spirituality by walking away from it. If we want to talk about salvage work or radical transformation it must be of our societies as well as ourselves. We cannot be made whole in isolation any more than we can set out to mend the world and ignore our own need for healing.

I can live with the paradox more easily now but I have learned to do so from my own experiences of failure and betrayal and by making silly mistakes about the whole business. I have spent a lot of my life being a bit like Stevie Smith's cat, galloping about doing good and not understanding at all why angels stood in my path murmuring 'Poor Cat'.[5] Religious people, as Jesus observed with his own splendid irony, are very good at charging about removing specks of dust from other people's eyes and fail-

8

ing to see the plank of wood sticking out of their own. I can see now how often I used religion as a retreat from reality, a way of running away from life and my own problems or simply as a way of feeling slightly superior.

Some years ago I came across the following in Gerald Priestland's autobiography:

> There is no such thing as religious experience — just experience. Love makes sense and purpose of life but you must trust yourself to it.[6]

I must have been feeling rather down in the dumps or over-exposed to Quaker dualisms on that particular day for I almost stood and cheered when I read it. It resonated with my experience and I wanted to add that there is no such thing as 'religious' life either. There are only the exercises of faith and the disciplines we choose for ourselves to open up our lives to God's love and the inward work of the spirit. If they do not make us more fully human and alive in every sense of the word we are on the wrong track or into the business of protecting ourselves from life.

I am not suggesting that all my friends in religious orders are not really living. They know as well as I do that the world is in their hearts, not left behind when they chose to join a particular community of faith. Their life together contains the same mixture of joy and grief, conflicts and anxiety, as well as the complexities of living with others and with themselves.

I thought it was vintage Priestland when I first jotted down the quotation from *Something Understood*. It sounded like him. When I came to check it I found that the words were notes of some of the things said by George Gorman at a weekend for enquirers at Charney Manor. There is something fitting about using them at this point. Some of what I have written in this book has grown from the experience of living in the larger-than-life shadow of George Gorman. I have tried to do, in my own way, the job that was his before it was handed on to me.

9

For those who relished his enormous capacity for friendship, his remarkable sensitivity to the mood of the 'sixties' and the needs of enquirers, and his single hearted efforts to make the Society known to twentieth-century seekers, I must have been something of a shock. I have seen my contribution quite differently. My priorities have been to build up a larger team to share the heavy responsibilities which George Gorman, and a much smaller team, carried between them, and to work more closely with Woodbrooke in providing resources for adult learning. I am more of a hermit by temperament and need large chunks of silence and solitude to recharge my internal batteries. Perhaps this is one of the reasons for my opting to belong to a society which values both silence and friendship, and sees itself in the apostolic succession of those who were friends of Jesus before they were sent out to spell out the meaning of it.

*   *   *

The word 'God' is as shop-soiled as the word 'spiritual'. It has been abused and distorted in much the same way. Part of me would like to declare a moratorium on religious language for a very long time. I know that if we did we would find ourselves inventing new metaphors, new code words to symbolise the mystery which we sense at the heart of our existence in an astonishing universe. I suspect that Martin Buber was right when he suggested that although '. . . . the word "God" is soiled and mutilated, it is for this very reason that we dare not abandon it. It cannot be cleansed or made whole by us 'but we can at least raise it from the ground and set it over an hour of great concern'.[7]

I know that for some Friends the word 'God' has been so broken and mutilated that they find it hard to use. Some of them have been damaged by over-exposure to bad religion. They have suffered too much from those who, in the name of God, have tried to bully others into accepting their view of reality. God has been used as a three-line whip to ensure their proper response to spiritual or moral issues.

Others have been so browbeaten and conditioned by religious dogmatism or literal interpretations of the Bible that they find it hard to let go of any images of God which do not speak to them. Meister Eckhart's 'for God's sake taking leave of God'[8] has seemed too much like high treason to allow them to take a 'holiday from God' or give themselves a breathing space to find new metaphors for that mystery. They go on flinching at the word and leave their bruises unexplored. And some Friends believe they have outgrown the metaphor completely.

The language that Christians have borrowed and pressed into service to try and express their experiences of encounter with the holy is now causing us such difficulty that we become hesitant about using it all. Our diffidence often extends to an equally uneasy reticence about borrowing new metaphors from science or psychology which might take us further into the heart of what we can never fully understand or translate into words.

Our habit of silence is powerful. Our reticence may, or may not, be a healthy wisdom about not trying to name the mystery. There is wisdom for the garrulous in the words of the Tao te Ching:

> Those who know do not talk
> Those who talk do not know[9]

But I cannot tell the story of my heart and leave God out of it. As I look back over my life it seems to have been crammed with beatitude and green epiphanies. I know that I have been, as Muslim friends would say, 'a guest of God' and the hospitality has been lavish even when, like the author of Psalm 23, I have felt ringed by hostile critics or walked alone through some dark valley of the shadow. It seems that love was waiting for me at every turn of the road and with me even when I was least aware of it.

I have used the word 'God' because I cannot think of a better one to stand as a symbol for the Mystery I sense at the heart of this vast and astonishing universe; and for that sense of a holy presence that has played hide and seek with me in all my journeying. I know it is only a crude shorthand for a mystery which defies my stammering efforts to describe it. I would have the same difficulty in trying to describe any of the relationships that have so enriched my life.

During the past eight and a half years of visiting Meetings and staying in Quaker homes I have talked with Friends who confess, with the honesty which is somehow one of our stubborn characteristics, that they find the idea of a personal God a very difficult one to entertain. They believe that our more sophisticated knowledge about the origins of life has made any anthropomorphic concepts of God obsolete.

I have chosen to express my awareness of God in personal terms simply because at the deepest level of my being I am conscious of being addressed by a presence which I can only define as 'Another', a 'Thou' which is somehow part of me, and also beyond me; or as Paul puts it in his letter to the church in Rome a 'God in whom we live and move and have our being'.[10] Even if I were not part of the Christian tradition, in which the essential nature of that 'other' inclusive presence has been fleshed out for us in a human life, I think I would have to describe my encounters in terms which include the personal. There have been too many surprising synchronisities and loving conspiracies in my life for me to dismiss that sense of a holy presence and a gracious host/ess.

Friends have played with a number of metaphors to symbolise their sense of God at work within them. We have spoken about having an inward teacher, the spirit, the inward light, of the 'seed' of Godness implanted in our lives because of one who allowed his life to be broken open and fall into darkness before it became green with promise.

In a new age we may want to find different ways of expressing our sense of the holy. Death and Resurrection are not simply built into the fabric of our mythologies or experienced in our individual journeys. They are built into the structure of the universe. In the brilliant dying of stars we can trace the evolution of new worlds. In the exploration of our human potential or the Jungian path of individuation we can find the same images of going down into darkness and being re-birthed, or energy being transmuted into new forms of being.

What I have written about my own journey from light into darkness and back again is a description, not a prescription for anyone else. Unearthing our buried treasure and learning to love the world in our hearts is our own work. No one else can do it for us or tell us exactly how to go about it. But I have always been grateful to those whose stories encouraged me to do my own excavating.

Chapter 2
Year of Jubilee

... This is the use of memory
For liberation—not less of love but expanding
Of love beyond desire, and so liberation
From the future as well as the past.[1]
T. S. Eliot, 'Little Gidding', *Four Quartets.*

... in the end the least misleading ikon is to be
found, not in the physical world outside us,
but in the human heart. The best analogy is ...
our experience of caring intensely for another
person, and of knowing that our love is
returned.[2]
Kallistos Ware, *The Orthodox Church.*

There is a time for the evening under starlight
A time for the evening under lamplight
(The evening with the photograph album).[3]
T. S. Eliot, 'East Coker', *Four Quartets.*

Turning back the pages of my life I have been surprised by
moments of vision, still vivid in memory, still ringed with
light. I have never, consciously, wanted to hoard or hold
onto them. I thought they belonged only to the past. Nor
did I expect repeat performances. It seemed to me at the
time that they were given for particular moments of need or
summoning, as preparation for new and difficult work or as
revision for lessons I failed to understand the first time. I
never regarded them as spiritual trophies, or as any more
significant than the day to day business of commitment and
obligation.

William Littleboy reminds us that 'To be a Christian con-
sists not in feeling but in following: not in ecstasy but in
obedience.'[4] Nowadays I am more uneasy about the
relation between obedience and love. It seems a curious
word to use about our relationship to God and it does not
occur very much in the context of the Gospels.

14

In the Jewish calendar the fiftieth year in every cycle of fifty was celebrated as the year of Jubilee. It was sometimes called the year of liberty because during the course of it old debts were written off, mortgaged land was restored to its owners and bonded servants were set free. During that period of reflection and celebration the Jewish people were encouraged to remember their past deliverance from slavery in Egypt and their special responsibility to be a community of peace and justice.

1963 will always have a place in my album of memories as a year of Jubilee, a time of liberation and beginning all over again.

It was the year in which the deans of three Cambridge colleges and a professor of divinity delivered four remarkable lectures, published immediately under the title *Objections to Christian Belief*. Two of the Cambridge four had already written controversial essays in *Soundings* published in the previous year. Lotte and Werner Pelz had written an astounding book *God is No More* and in the same year Paul van Buren's *The Secular Meaning of the Gospel* became a best seller on both sides of the Atlantic. *Towards a Quaker View of Sex* hit the headlines and *Honest to God* became top of the pops among religious paperbacks in this country. Rachel Carson's *Silent Spring* published in 1962 was already preparing the way for the Green revolution and an eighty-two year old Pope, dying of cancer, was presiding over a Council which threw open the windows and doors of the Catholic world and let the winds of the Spirit blow through them at gale force. He died on June 3rd of my year of Jubilee, a few weeks after completing his magnificent *Pacem in Terris* (Peace on Earth).

*   *   *

I open the album for 1963 and snapshots tumble out, some in black and white but most in colour that is still unfaded. There is one of a Deaconess, dignified in navy-blue with a prim white collar and cuffs. I am on my way to a retreat which will bring the primness to an abrupt halt. In my briefcase are the books I have mentioned already, required reading for the weekend.

The next photograph is one I treasure most. It is of the leader of the retreat walking alone on the sands at Saltburn. I am on the cliffs looking down. I know with that sudden intuitive knowledge of the heart that this person will change my life as irrevocably as reading those books. I do not know then that we shall one day share a home and that in it I shall learn the meaning of God's love. Until that time I had thought, as many religious people do, that divine and human love were quite different things, the human variety only a pale reflection of the other. Now I know, as Dante did, that it is so often through those we love that the gates of new life are opened and we are brought home to the place where we belong.

I pick up another snapshot and smile at one of God's jokes. I am writing late at night in a dark-blue notebook, 'I am going to become a Quaker.' I write page after page about why I believe that Friends have the kind of spiritual open house which enables them to offer hospitality and space in their worship to twentieth-century seekers. I am thinking about the students and young people with whom I work but my own needs are part of the picture too. I do not know then that the journey will take me another fifteen years.

A few more pictures tumble out as I turn the pages. There is one of me looking unusually smart and slim in a white silk dress with black polka dots and wearing a large white hat. I am one of the official representatives of British Methodism at the second annual Conference of the newly independent Methodist Church of Ghana. I remember the dress chiefly because I seem to become accident prone whenever I wear it. I have worn it twice before, once to a garden party at Lambeth Palace where I lost my umbrella and then to a reception of national youth leaders at St James' Palace. At the latter a maid spilt fruit cup down the front of it. I had to hide behind a pillar when the royals arrived. Now I am in Accra, responding to the most curious welcome ever given to a 'Deaconess in the Church of God', at a time when that implied life-long celibacy. My interpreter has just whispered to me the concluding words of my official Ghanaian welcome—'Go well, O one ripe for marriage'. As I rise to my feet torn between amusement and discomfort, to make a suitable response I can feel the tops of my new independent suspension stockings beginning to slip, wrinkle and slide slowly and inexorably downwards. My one and only venture into sartorial elegance comes to an ignominious halt around my ankles.

The next picture is stark, in black and white. It is a close-up of some passengers crossing the tarmac at Heathrow airport. I am seeing the faces of affluent westerners as if for the first time. They are mirror reflections of my own. For the past five weeks I have been given a whistle-stop tour of Ghana. I have seen the Ghana of the twentieth-century with its Wimpey buildings and its equivalent of the Dorchester. I have walked through the shanty towns around Accra. I have been driven along the red earth roads north of Kumasi, through villages which seem not far removed from the stone age. I have visited tiny mission hospitals and the school for blind children at Wa. I have seen for myself the human faces behind the statistics of third world deprivation about which I have talked so often to student groups and youth clubs. I have met and learned from those whose deprivation has been my theme.

I have also seen the other side which the Oxfam posters do not show. The hunger and poverty are real and terrible enough. Yet in the midst of them I have heard songs and laughter. I have watched women and men and children dancing their faith, celebrating their life and thanking God for the gift of it. This close-up of western faces reminds me of that moment of vision on the tarmac at Heathrow airport when I caught a glimpse of a different kind of deprivation which haunts the eyes of those of us who live in what we have chosen to call civilisation. It flickers on the anxious faces of those of us who have lost our sense of connection with the earth and of living in communities which have a sense of past, future and present, the living and the dead, intimately bound together. We are dying in a different way

because we have lost our capacity for wonder and celebration and no longer know how to dance our faith without
embarrassment or sing the songs of freedom with any
sense of our need of it.

Oxfam posters, United Nations Reports, TV newsreels
and documentaries, long conversations with those who
work in under-developed areas, have all prepared me, to
some extent, for the shock of seeing children dying of mal-
nutrition and disease. Nothing has prepared for this flight
back to my old world and the vision of the 'Waste Land'.
Words from the Wisdom literature of the Jewish world flash
into my shocked mind — 'where there is no vision the
people perish.' I know that nothing will ever be quite the
same again. I am like some stranded survivor of a great sea
change, no longer at ease in the world I left five weeks
before.

The last few photographs in my 1963 album are an odd
collection; a room in the Student Christian Movement
headquarters at Annandale, a group of students from Leicester University, an SCM field secretary giving me a copy of
*Christian Faith and Practice in the Experience of the Society of
Friends*. They belong to the last three months of my year of
Jubilee, between my old life as a professional religious,
struggling to use ways of prayer and books on Christian
spirituality which no longer reflect my experience and a
new life which is summed up in the words of W. H. Auden.

To discover how to be human now
is the reason we follow the star.[5]

In September of that momentous year I leave my job as
Youth Secretary at the Methodist Missionary Society. In
response to an invitation from Ambrose Reeves, ex Bishop
of Johannesburg, I join the staff at Annandale as one of his
two assistant general secretaries. My job is a mixture of
administration and visiting student groups to talk about
Christian faith and its relevance to problems of injustice
and deprivation. My first weekend conference is with a
group of students from Leicester University, the first of
many in which the questions of students seem to highlight

my own predicament. They talk about the search for reality in religion and their difficulties with institutional Christianity. So much of it seems to them to be incomprehensible, irrelevant or just boring. They cannot relate to it and I know how they feel.

They are critical of churches which seem to be authoritarian, dogmatic, obsessed with the problem of sexual morality and with their own maintenance and survival. I can understand their criticism as well as their complaints about sentimental hymns which express attitudes of fear, submission and dependency which no sensitive or caring parents would wish to encourage in their children. They sense behind the morbid sentimentality of Victorian hymns and the anguished entreaties of the *Book of Common Prayer* a picture of God which is repugnant to them. They cannot understand why the church should want to market the idea of God as a boorish tyrant or a rather unpleasant kind of cosmic boss.

I listen to their protests. I have my own problems with these primitive and patriarchal images of God, potent because they are buttressed by thousands of years of religious history, by uncritical views of scripture and by our own fear of freedom. Like these students I find it hard to understand why the church has failed to jettison views of God, or power structures, which find no support in the Gospel records. I can remind them of Christians who *have* understood the revolutionary nature of the Gospel but I cannot defend an institution which does not seem willing to be vulnerable or give much of its life away for others.

I find myself talking to them about other options which may be open to them. I suggest that for some of them the Society of Friends may be able to offer them a free and uncluttered space in which they can pursue their spiritual quest. I know it has a good track record when it comes to doing the faith rather than talking about it. It has the kind of pragmatic mysticism that appeals to me, and decision-making is a shared responsibility. I am twenty years away from my own immersion in Quaker institutionalism and still able to keep my romantic view of it.

The last photograph is slightly out of focus. I cannot remember where it was taken. It shows a girl with red hair giving me a copy of *Christian Faith & Practice*. I cannot remember whether we had talked about the Society of Friends very much. I must have said something about my sense of being drawn to it. Carolyn cannot know, as she gives me this book, that I shall one day work in the place where it is published, or that it will be part of my job to introduce it to others who are not yet Friends. The book she has given me will become important to me but it will lie unopened for several years because there are other things I must do first.

Towards the end of the year I know that I have reached a turning point. I need a space in which to think through all the implications of this year of grace. I ask for a period of sabbatical leave and in the autumn of 1964 I begin to write and paint and reflect on what has happened to me. I want to explore the possibilities of Art Therapy. I am drawn to the ministry of writing. One door at least is open to me. I manage to secure a place in Leeds College of Art and for the next four years become a student again. One of the students in my year is a Friend. Her father teaches art at Wennington School where Kenneth Barnes is Headmaster. For years I have recommended his *He and She* to young people. It is one of the sanest books on sexuality that I know. Is it coincidence or a gracious synchronicity?

At the end of those four years I become a research fellow teaching in the Department of Communication Design in Leeds Polytechnic and exploring the ways in which visual communication can be used to stimulate creativity in children with serious learning difficulties. Eventually I shall move on to work with children in special schools. They will never become 'yuppies' or high-flyers. Our success-orientated society has no place for them. It has chosen to label them as maladjusted, handicapped and socially deprived. To work among those who have been marginalised seems an appropriate way of extending a ministry of teaching and healing, though in the end I think I learned more from them than the other way round. I find myself so much at home with them that I do not expect to leave this particular sphere of service. Only a very strong sense of inward compulsion prompts me, in 1980, to reply to an advertisement in *The Friend* which results in my coming to work for Quakers. I am very surprised that they are willing to take the risk of appointing someone who has been a member of the Society for only two years.

Coming to work for Friends after twelve years of working with under-privileged children is another tremendous shock, almost as great as the shock of returning from Ghana. I find myself in a different world, working with those who are generally, but not entirely, thank God, very privileged people. I do not expect to find vast tracts of the waste land here, but of course I do. Friends are often as handicapped as I have been, and still am, by being too cerebral and still in the kindergarten where the education of feelings is concerned.

I look back at the year in which I stepped out of one world and into another. It remains in my memory, and I suspect in the memory of many of my generation, as a time of miracles, a little springtime of the spirit for those of us who had felt oppressed and alienated by the religious institutions to which we belonged.

Now, in 1990, as I walk across the concourse at Euston station on my way to Friends House I wonder what happened to that rumour of springtime in the churches with its counterpart in Flower Power and the harlequin colours of the Hippie scene. I am not defending the excesses of the latter or the way in which the movement was later exploited but I grieve at what has happened since. Young people are dressed more often now in sombre black, mourning perhaps for that lost springtime. I see young people, and children, begging as they have not needed to since the days when Dickens wrote about the forlorn flotsam of Victorian society, begging as I once saw the children of African shanty towns doing. In spite of liberation and renewal movements there is a touch of frost in the air and perhaps the frozen helplessness I feel as I dispense my awkward charity is my only link with these bleak children of the nineties.

This book, which began to germinate in that lost spring-time, has been completed in a colder climate. Religious institutions seem to be suffering, at least in some quarters, from a hardening of the oughteries. A new puritanism is emerging which wants to control and tidy up, to draw hard lines of demarcation between insiders and outsiders. Religious and Biblical dogmatism is resurgent, and com-passion is low on the agenda of a society which is obsessed with market values.

In spite of the chill winds of what sometimes feels like a time of spiritual recession there are signs of hope in unexpected places. Our world has changed dramatically since I began to write this book. No one was dancing on the Berlin Wall then and the Green party was viewed as a romantic aberration or a bunch of doom and gloom fanat-ics. A new revolution is under way, breaking down walls, opening up frontiers and new possibilities of co-operation in a way that few of us expected to see in our lifetime.

There are things that the Spirit is saying to people of faith and hope in every religious tradition. Something is hap-pening, and some of us are picking up the signals of a new age. I suspect that there will be no complete paragraphs of hope until we have learned how to share our resources.

The God with whom we have to do is always our contem-porary. Perhaps that is why some of the signals we hear are not transmitted to us in yesterday's language. I am not pre-tending to be any less hard of hearing than most of us but it seems to me that the Biblical tradition to which dogmatists would like us to return is very clear at this point. There is no going back. We are a pilgrim people who must take to the road again, learning as we go to sing a new song and to trust the God who is always bringing new things to birth.

Biblical dogmatists who are part of the new puritanism seem to believe that faith is simply a matter of turning back to the Bible to find within it clear and unequivocal answers to every human problem. I have sometimes heard them talking as if those of us who do not use the Bible in that par-ticular way are somehow lacking in faith or want an easy ride.

In my experience trying to walk by faith has much more to do with doubt and uncertainty and the kind of basic trust in God which enables us to manage quite well without a complete set of instructions. We used to sing a hymn which encapsulates that kind of confidence:

> By Thine unerring spirit led
> We shall not in the desert stray
> We shall not full direction need
> Nor miss our providential way
> As far from danger as from fear
> While Love, almighty Love is near.[6]

Walking by faith does not seem to me to be about having certain knowledge that you are on the right track or being able to see the way ahead quite clearly. Sometimes it seems to involve making a path where there was not one before. I am not a very bold person. I find going off the beaten track fairly unnerving. Contrary to popular views of religion having faith seems to involve a lot of insecurity and becoming free has its own kind of anxieties and loneliness. It is often not at all comfortable and certainly not an easy option.

When I first read J. Neville Ward's reflections on the Lord's prayer *Beyond Tomorrow.* I was arrested by some words in the introduction in which he writes:

> The Lord's prayer must have come from Jesus'
> inner world, where he was truly himself, an
> insecure, loving man, prepared to take the risk
> of loving.[7]

In fact the words of it were gleaned from prayers which belonged to the Jewish liturgy but I am sure that Neville Ward is right about the fact that they had become part of his inner world and the self-possession which enabled him to live the tensions between insecurity and trust. 1963 remains a year of Jubilee for me because it was in that year that I learned to doubt and trust and to take the risks of love.

Chapter 3
Knowing Experimentally

The moment of vision, although it's a fresh individual experience for all of us, gains its power because it is a morsel of collective experience as well. The poet and artist, born as we all are with a capacity for delighted self-discovery in certain symbols, finds amongst them a few which outlive his childhood because they nourish the centre of his creative being.[1]

Kenneth Clarke, *Moments of Vision*

Now I was come up in the spirit through the flaming sword into the paradise of God. All things were new, and all creation gave another smell unto me beyond what words can utter.[2]

George Fox, *Journal*

Truthfully I say to you, whoever does not receive the kingdom of God like a child shall not enter it.[3]

Luke, 18.v.17

The child is alone for the first time in a field of bright grasses. The grass is tall. It reaches above her shoulders. She is submerged in light, standing on uncertain feet in a field of green and gold, a toddler in paradise. The grass sings. It flashes like the fire of a million emeralds, her small heart contracts with the terror of separation and then expands to fill the universe. She is no longer intimately connected to one human being. She is somehow connected to everything in the universe, full of it, into it, part of it. For one shining moment she and the universe are one.

Minutes pass. Time passes. The child is no longer in time. The grasses swell and surge like the movement of a great ocean of light. She walks in the light, runs in it, swims in it, is part of the dancing and no longer afraid.

A cloud goes over the sun. A shadow falls on the bright world. The mother's voice calls anxiously. The child is aware of loneliness, cries, and stumbles back into time. But she does not forget the ocean of light in a field of bright grasses.

Quaker spirituality is about awareness and inward knowing. It is about becoming aware of the real issues of life whether we are thinking about the pollution or nuclear devastation of our planet, about poverty or oppression or about the impoverishment of our inner lives. It is about peace and reconciliation in both our inner and outer worlds. Our social awareness begins with our awareness of dissonance or harmony within. This is the starting point for Friends simply because all that is happening on our planet is the giant shadow of a drama being played out on the inside of our lives.

George Fox understood this very well when he wrote in his journal in 1647 'And I went back to Nottinghamshire, and the Lord showed me that the natures of those things which were hurtful without, were within . . . '[4] Most of his contemporaries were busy blaming other people for the social unrest and dislocation in their society but what follows in his journal makes it clear that he had discovered, to his own surprise and horror, that the roots of violence and destructiveness were located in his own heart.

The primacy of personal experience is another important aspect of our spirituality. It includes our knowledge that evil and good are entwined in the depths of our own being and also the glorious affirmation that we are children of light, created from the brilliant explosions of dying stars.

For George Fox it was natural to identify his experience of inward knowing with metaphors gleaned from the biblical tradition; seed, light, spirit, Christ or God. All that he knew experimentally he believed to be the direct result of having discovered Christ as his inward tutor.

Janet Scott, in the foreword to her 1980 Swarthmore Lecture *What Cans't Thou Say?* reminds us of the three disturbing questions which George Fox put to the congregation at Ulverston Church in 1652. The first is well

25

known to Friends: 'You will say Christ saith this, and the apostles say this; but what cans't thou say?' The next two are less familiar to Friends, some of whom might like to believe that George Fox was giving us a charter for spiritual anarchy or idiosyncratic religion: 'Art thou a child of light and hast walked in the light?' and 'What thou speakest is it inwardly from God?'[5]

It has taken me years to understand how important those questions are. I am not as clear as some Friends seem to be about the process of discernment involved in being able to say a confident 'yes' to the third. I know the questions are crucial ones. It has taken me half a lifetime to realise that a great deal that has been written about Christian spirituality makes no sense to me at all. Some of what George Fox wrote in the seventeenth century makes very little sense to me as a woman in the latter half of the twentieth century. I would not expect it to do so. But his questions have prompted me to become aware of my different experience as a woman, the things I know experimentally, and to dig deeper to unearth the things I know in the hidden places in my own life.

I can understand why some women are angry that the church has devalued their experiences and burdened them with unhelpful models of spirituality. But I do not want to blame the church for adopting and adapting a pattern of Christian devotion designed originally by celibate males and monastic drop-outs in the fourth and fifth centuries. I do not blame myself either for being slow to trust my own insights and 'openings'. What would be the point? Besides, it is not all loss. I have relished the wisdom of the Desert Fathers, and Mothers. I love the Zen-like quality of their sayings. I respect the courage and faith of those who dropped out of a dying civilisation to create alternative societies capable of sustaining hope. There are times when I go to Matins or Compline and value this sense of continuity with the past.

But I am not a male monastic or an anchorite. I live in a world in which the wilderness is never far away. I can appreciate new forms of community or counter-cultures.

26

But I need to make my own prayers and express my faith in a language that reflects my different experiences. It is bound to be different. Yesterday's language of faith belongs to a different time and place and it rests on assumptions and preconceptions about God which I do not have.

Religious people seem to find it hard to abandon past practices or old images of God, as if there were something blasphemous or faithless in doing so. I am not dishonouring the past or negating the wisdom of ancient tradition. But I cannot live on spiritual hand-me-downs no matter how grand, antique or elevated they may be. I have discovered, in my slow and laborious way, 'like a dormouse on valium' (as they say of American comedian, Stephen Wright) that it is perilously easy to use religious practices as a way of dodging reality or opting out of the difficult business of living with other people and myself. Spirituality may be about God-knowing but it includes the more complicated enterprise of getting to know yourself. I shall say more about this in a later chapter.

What does it mean for us as Friends to know experimentally? I like Douglas Steere's description of Quaker meetings as 'laboratories of the Holy Spirit'.[6] A laboratory is a place for investigation and experiment, whether it happens to be yourself or God who is studied in depth. There is nothing fixed or final about what happens in a laboratory. Jocelyn Burnell, in the 1989 Swarthmore Lecture *Broken for Life* reminds us that scientists explore some aspect of the universe by inventing models or pictures which are useful for their exploration but also have their limitations. They are provisional and may have to be jettisoned as new discoveries are made. Mistakes are part of the process of investigation. Nothing matters but the determination to go on making and discarding provisional models until we come to the point of understanding and knowing.

Every Quaker meeting has that kind of potential. It allows us the space for a real experiment in depth. In it we are exploring a mystery—the mystery of who we are in relation to a very much bigger mystery and what our partial understanding involves us in doing about it. Friends talk a lot about 'gathered meetings' and the business of 'centring down'. I am not sure that it happens often, but I have been in meetings in which we were open to God and to one another, in which our silent waiting on God and our loving attention seemed to bring us to a place of deeper understanding. A few Friends spoke from the centre of themselves in a way that touched that core of being in all of us and we knew that the place in which we were sitting had become holy ground. I don't know how it happens but I suspect that fear and lack of compasssion for one another are powerful inhibitors and that it could happen much more often if we had the courage to be open and real with one another. I have been in meetings in which the ministry was powerful and healing simply because one member had allowed some of their inner destitution to be exposed to others.

*   *   *

There are some Friends who talk about the processes of enlightenment or inward knowing as if they begin only at the moment of conversion and could then be expected to unfold during private prayer or in a gathered meeting. What we know experimentally or on the inside of our lives does not seem to me to be about religious experience or pious practices, though the latter may nourish our capacity for greater awareness. I find it puzzling, and sometimes exasperating, when religious institutions behave as though they have some kind of monopoly of transcendent experiences or the right to erect religious fencing round our deepest moments of awareness. It is as if they thought of themselves as the largest shareholders in a company exporting mystical knowledge! In fact the church has been very suspicious or opppressive about unmediated experiences of grace. Some of my aversion to this kind of possessiveness and categorising springs from the fact that my inward knowing began long before I set foot in a church and some of the most gathered meetings I have known have taken place in unexpected places, among people who did not have any formal association with religious institutions.

There is nothing exceptional about the fact that adults or children may have transcendent experiences long before they have any religious framework into which they can be incorporated and many have no desire to fit them into existing structure of belief. Friends, as a rule, have fewer problems at this point than some Christian groups because their basic beliefs rest on the assumption that there is 'that of God' in all human beings and the process of inward enlightenment is not dependent on the mediation of spiritual guides or experts.

Martin Israel tells us that at the age of three he had a vivid awareness of his destiny. He knew that he was called to be a prophetic preacher, a healer and a spiritual counsellor; and that his journey would include a great deal of darkness. 'In my life' he writes, 'the call came very early. I was not more than three years old when I heard, with the inward ear, a voice that addressed me directly in the darkness of my inner self, yet it carried with it a radiant light. It gave me a preview of the pattern of my life, and showed me the path I had to follow to be an authentic person.'[7]

Martin Israel confesses that he expects his readers to be incredulous. He expects them to dismiss his childhood 'knowing' as too fantastic to be taken seriously. I found myself wondering why. Why should we assume that a child's perception of reality is less reliable than our adult view of it? Why should we assume that our adult, rational-way of looking at the world is inevitably superior to the ways in which we see and know in childhood? Do we assume that our western educational systems or Piaget and other developmental psychologists have got it right and that we can dismiss as Jewish hyperbole what Jesus said about the need to become like children before we can step into the kingdom of reality.

I have no difficulty in accepting the veracity of Martin Israel's memory of childhood knowing. At the age of three I knew one of the most important things about the universe and my place in it. The experience I have tried to describe at the beginning of this chapter was as real to me as Martin Israel's sense of calling was to him. And from the thousands of accounts sent to the Religious Experience Research Unit at Manchester College, Oxford, it is clear that my childhood experience was not unusual. Many of those who wrote in could recall similar moments of knowing in which the world was transfigured, or they saw it as it is in reality, and knew what Kenneth Boulding, in the *Naylor Sonnets*, describes as 'the burning Oneness binding everything.'[8]

Those who have researched this area of human experience have sometimes chosen rather grandiose ways of classifying it. They have written about altered states of consciousness, higher and lower consciousness, noetic or numinous experiences, moments of transcendence, cosmic consciousness or moments of cosmic disclosure. It is splendid stuff but I find myself resistant to this passion for labelling moments of awareness in this way. It is rather like taking a brilliant butterfly and killing it to make a museum exhibit. It also has the unfortunate effect of removing such moments from the common experience of human beings and making them sound much more rarified than they are.

I remember a thin, malnourished child in one of the small groups of children who came to me for remedial language classes. She stood at the window of the small room in which we held the classes watching the gulls from the estuary wheeling and diving over the school playing fields. After a moment she turned away, her eyes wide with wonder, and said 'Gawd Miss, ain't they lovely!' She must have seen, yet never really seen them many times before, but on that particular afternoon she opened her eyes and saw them as if for the first time.

I have never wanted to label that vivid moment of awareness in a field of bright grasses. At the age of three I had no conceptual models or religious frame of reference into which I could have fitted it. It was years before I read Wordsworth's 'Prelude', and I would protest vigorously if anyone tried to label it 'Wordsworthian'. I do not share Wordsworth's sense of irretrievable loss. I step in and out of eternity at all kinds of unexpected moments, and still have 'one foot in Eden'.[9] Nor will I allow the church to devalue such moments by calling them pantheist or even panentheist. 'The world is charged with the grandeur of God,'[10] as Hopkins knew, and the passion of more pedantic souls to try and pigeon-hole our awareness of that grandeur seems to me a sad and silly exercise. Moments of vision are just that, moments when like that small girl in my language class, we open our eyes and see!

Chapter 4

In and Out of Time

The boundaries of the human person are extremely wide; each of us knows very little about his true and deep self. Through our faculties of perception, outward and inward, through our memory and through the power of the unconscious, we range widely over space, we stretch backward and forward in time, and we reach out beyond space and time into eternity.[1]

Kallistos Ware, *The Orthodox Way*

Always at the commencement of work that first innocence must be achieved. You must return to that unsophisticated spot where the angel first discovered you when he brought the first binding message . . . If the angel deigns to come it will be because you have convinced him, not with tears, but with your humble resolve to be always beginning.[2]

Rainer Maria Rilke, *Letters to a Friend*

In the beginner's mind there are many possibilities but in the expert's there are few.[3]

Shunryu Suzuki, *Zen Mind, Beginner's Mind*

I am grateful that my exposure to formal religion was very low voltage for the first ten years of my life. It has given me a certain detachment and freedom to question which might have been difficult to achieve if I had been soaked in conventional Christianity from the beginning.

From my materal grandparents I learned how much violence and self-loathing can lurk behind pious words and practices. My mother had been born with a double curvature of the spine. She had been alternatively over-protected and bullied by her strict, respectable and church-going parents. She remembered her upright father beating her with a poker, projecting his horror of imperfection on to the back of his deformed child.

Having caught a glimpse of unhealthy religion and the difficulties which religious people have in becoming self-aware, I am sometimes amazed that I found my way into the church at all, and having got there, dived in at the deep end. I seem to be an 'all or nothing' kind of person and I was not interested in paddling. But having glimpsed the gap between profession and practice I have always been a bit sceptical and irreverent about religious life. I find myself over-reacting, often unfairly I suspect, to those who seem to specialise in pious utterance.

As a teenager I did the round of churches and mission halls, not from any spiritual hunger or religious fervour. I went with a school friend to spy out the best hunting grounds and a very peculiar clutch of spotty youths and eager amorists we managed to cull. On one of these hopeful expeditions we found ourselves at a large evangelical rally at the Dome, in Brighton. Two of the speakers were the kind who still give me goose pimples. The third speaker was a Franciscan friar. I do not remember what he said or what he looked like. I remember that he spoke very simply and quietly from some place deep within himself. No doubt his plain brown habit and air of stillness were sharp contrast to the pin-stripes, florid ties and heavy breathing of the two hot gospellers. At any rate he won the contest hands down. Friends would say he spoke to that of God within me. He did just that. He spoke from the centre of his life and it touched some deep place in my gawky, adolescent soul.

From that moment on I was hooked on God, and though I have sometimes wished I were not, nothing has ever undone that moment of saying 'yes'. I did not understand very clearly who or what I was saying yes to, but it changed the course of my life. I did not move forward with the crowds of would-be disciples who began to make their way to the front of the auditorium. Nothing in me felt that I wanted or needed to make that kind of gesture. But it was just as conclusive for me as if I had gone in for total immersion.

Never having had much exposure to the virus in my early life I caught religion badly. I stopped looking for likely lads and fell in love with God instead. It was much more satisfactory and romantic. His breath did not smell of chewing gum, garlic or menthol and He did not interrupt me when I wanted to talk about my ideas. God was definitely male for me in those days, the reliable father-figure who would not desert me by being declared 'missing, believed killed.'

I joined Donald Soper's 'Order of Christian Witness' and went out in great fear and timidity to evangelise post-war Britain, which was not very responsive. But it was good practice for a fledgling preacher. I became what Methodists call a local preacher and stunned my first congregation with a thirty minute sermon on the text 'It is good for me to have been afflicted'.[4] The congregation were kind. They may have felt that I had got it wrong about who was being afflicted but they made appreciative noises afterwards; (touched no doubt by the fact that I was young, enthusiastic, and in those far-off-days, easy on the eye). I went home mildly elated that I could indulge my passion for purple prose by being garrulous for God.

*   *   *

There are moments in our lives that have nothing to do with digital watches or the weeks, months and years that pass on the ordinary calendar of our lives. The Greeks were wise enough to have two words to distinguish one from the other: *Chronos* for the time that seems to flow in ordered sequences, measurable by our clocks and calendars and *Kairos* for the moment of grace and destiny.

Three moments in my life are ringed with fire on my inward calendar. There are other moments that are luminous in a different way but these three are the ones that belong to a different order of time which is part of the eternal present. The first is my primal experience of grace when I stood with both feet in Eden in a field of bright grasses. The third is the moment when I stood on a windswept cliff

in north Yorkshire and knew that I was intimately connected with another human being in a way that would change
my life and teach me the meaning of love.

The second is more difficult to describe. It contains those
elements of recognition and wonder which illuminated the
others. It includes the strange combination of mystery and
familiarity I associate with them, but it has its one curious
difference. Those who have had a near death experience
and returned to life tell us that they saw the event from a
point above the place where their physical body was lying. I
was very much alive but I had the same sense of watching
what was happening to me from a different place
altogether.

As a rule I have a poor visual memory of the clothes I
have been wearing at other significant moments in my life.
On this occasion I saw myself very clearly, standing in a
dark blue coat with a hood, in front of the altar-rail in the
church which had become important to me after my
father's death. It was the occasion of my recognition as a
local preacher in the Methodist Church. I cannot recall now
the details of the service or how large the congregation was.
Nor can I remember the face of the minister who conducted
it. The words of commissioning did not come from him and
the voice of that calling is not contained in any book.

*I am standing alone at the front of the church. It is an old Sussex
tithe barn with massive oak beams, salvaged it is claimed, from the
wrecks of Spanish ships at the time of the Armada. It is evening
and the high flint walls are barely illuminated by the candle-shaped
lamps on the uneven timbers that buttress them. I can see myself
standing in the place where, three hundred years or so before,
Sussex farmers came to offer a tenth of their yearly harvest.
Whether they brought their grain and sheep reluctantly or with
gratitude to God, I do not know. I know, as I watch myself standing, kneeling and waiting, that somehow, more is expected of me.*

The ancient tithe barn, reclaimed by nonconformists as a
place for worship, was demolished years ago. In its place is
a modern church of raw, red brick. But the moment remains

to puzzle me with its implications. Like Jeremiah, diffident
and ill at ease with his public role, I have sometimes wanted
to undo that moment of inner summoning. Thirty-eight
years later I am still awkward and unsuited to it. Yet nothing that has happened in those years has altered that
inward calling or the 'yes' of my life in response to it.
Becoming a Friend has not changed it in spite of the fact that
we no longer formally record Quaker ministers as we once
did. I felt no sense of betrayal in moving away from a situation in which I had exercised that ministry in more conventional ways. Instead, becoming a Friend has focused
that sense of calling in a different way and allowed me to
see it as part of a shared ministry, a priesthood of all
believers.

Which of us ever understands what our 'yes' to God will
mean'? I said it in that Sussex tithe barn, truthfully and full
of innocent misunderstanding. I was still only a fledgling
Christian, new to the church and brimming over with adolescent enthusiasm to be a holy person, a woman of God.

I read all the books about Christian spirituality that I
could lay my hands on. I ransacked second-hand bookshops for copies of the spiritual classics, *The Confessions of St
Augustine*, *The Imitation of Christ*, William Law's *Call to a
Devout and Holy Life*, *The Little Flowers of St Francis*. My bookshelves still groan with the weight of all the manuals of
devotion and guides to the spiritual life that I collected in
those days.

In the post-Robinson era they seem so alien to us. We
have difficulty with their awkward dualisms and other-
worldliness. They bristle with assumptions that are no
longer tenable. But as I read them then, their message
seemed plain enough. They were based on the premise that
the only appropriate response to a God who gave his only
Son to suffer a peculiarly brutal death for our sakes was to
show our gratitude by relinquishing all right to a life of our
own. The way to do this seemed to be by a curious process
of turning our back on the world with all its distracting
beauty and also on any intimate relationships with human
beings. Those who wanted to go all out for God were appar-

ently required to say 'no' to almost everything that is pleasurable and satisfying to us as human beings.

It seems very strange to me now that I did not sense the dissonance between biblical affirmations about the goodness and breathtaking wonder of creation and the spiritual disciplines which applauded the idea of turning away from it and keeping your eyes firmly shut, or at least decently lowered, in case the blue fire of a kingfisher's wing or the fall of light on leaves or on a beloved face should distract you from your devotions.

Nor did I see immediately the contradiction between reciting creeds about the resurrection of the body and the flesh-taking of God, and the deep suspicion of the body which characterises the writing of some of the best known spiritual guides. No introduction to them ever took the trouble to place those strange, unwholesome aspirations in their historical context. Contemporary writers quoted them with approval. But I was a relative newcomer to the church and deep into its dualisms before I knew where I was.

I knew very little about the church, apart from my own small bit of it, and the books I read. For just over a decade the church had been my family, more solid and safe than the one broken and changed by bereavement. I was eager to prove to myself, to God and to my new community that I was serious about discipleship, though it never occurred to me to be a real monastic. When I became a student Deaconess, later in the same year as my recognition as a local preacher, I even managed to look the part I was playing. In return for donating my life to God I was entitled to wear a prim grey uniform with a stiff white collar and cuffs. After my ordination it would be navy blue. The up-market version today is a French blue, Hardy Amies design. I looked much more devastating in the old model. It gave me the look that choir boys often have, angelic and far too good to be true. It was very misleading to several probationer ministers, and at least two missionaries on furlough, who had been nudged by their superiors into looking round for a suitable partner. Foolishly they thought that I would make an ideal parson's wife. One of them wrote me a long letter informing me that he had it direct from the Lord that I was to be his chosen partner, and adding, somewhat ambiguously I thought, that he 'must have a wife who is always on her knees.'

I was not much into self-awareness in those days. Fortunately I had just about enough to see through my own disguise. I wrote back, as gently as I could, to make it clear that I, unfortunately, had not received a similar message and took that to mean that God had other plans for me.

It seems ungracious to put it all as crudely as I have done. Perhaps I needed that feeling of being different, and chosen. I shall always be profoundly grateful for that period in my life when I was preparing myself for service as a 'Deaconess in the Church of God.' I was accepted and believed in at a time when I was not very good at believing in myself. I enjoyed being in a company of women. I was free to spend hours and days in study and prayer, to worship in a community and have regular times for silent retreat. I remember there was a lot of laughter and fun as well as long, enthusiastic discussions about the future of the church.

I owe a tremendous debt to my tutors in biblical and pastoral theology. I do not believe we ever had a dull lecture from any of them. They made the Bible and the Christian story come alive for me and introduced me to more of the diversity and richness of Christian spirituality. It was during one of our college Quiet Days that I discovered Thomas Kelly's *Testament of Devotion* and Douglas Steere's Swarthmore Lecture *Where Words Come From*. In tutorials and seminars I came into contact with Julian of Norwich and Thomas Traherne. Baron von Hugel and Jean-Pierre de Caussade spoke to me in different ways. They were healthy correctives to the morbid aspects of monasticism. I discovered Janet Erskine Stuart who was an ardent naturalist, a life loving human being, who saw the world with a poet's eye and taught her novices with a splendid mix of robust common sense and lyricism. To a novice who was straining after impossible perfection she said 'Sit your saddle more loosely,'[5] advice that I have needed for most of my life.

It was in those privileged days of prayer and study that I first heard of the ecumenical movement, the Iona Community, the House Church, the *Kirchentag* and the French worker priest movement. The latter became an important influence in my thinking about the church in the world. We discussed these signs of a new age for hours over cups of coffee or the washing up.

*　　*　　*

I shall never qualify as a champion feminist. Whatever I now find to be difficult or alien to me in the long patriarchal bias of Christianity I cannot reject those days when I wanted to be, not my own woman at all, but God's, content to live in holy obedience for the rest of my life. The fact that I now interpret those words differently and see no contradiction between taking responsibility for my life and being a friend of God is not a recantation.

A few years ago a friend and I were visiting Meaux sur Marne. We went, as no doubt all visitors do, to see the twelfth-century cathedral of St Etienne. I can still remember the shock of its bare windows which should have been a blaze of colour like those of Notre Dame or Chartres. They were smashed to pieces by some of my Huguenot ancestors when they sacked the cathedral in 1560. I stood in the south porch and looked at the mutilated carvings in the tympanium. I felt a terrible sense of shame at the savage destruction of so much grace. There is something barbaric in the zeal of iconoclasts. It makes me apprehensive about the reforming passion of feminist extremists, as well as my own iconoclastic tendencies.

*　　*　　*

In the sixties my safe but claustrophobic religious world was broken open. Perhaps I no longer needed that kind of security. I caught a glimpse of how much of life I had been running away from in my attempt to be a dutiful handmaid of the Lord. I was shocked that I had accepted so much that now seemed to me morbid and unhealthy in my desire to live in holy obedience. Why on earth had I ever thought that a nurturing, creative God was all that keen on obedience anyway? Obviously it had far more to do with the social control exercised by an authoritarian church. It seemed to have very little to do with the revolutionary relationships of the Gospel order. Why had I allowed myself to believe that seeking the commonwealth of God involved constant self-abnegation and fear of being intimately involved with others? Walking in the shanty towns around Accra and listening to the crying of hungry children made the whole idea of perfecting my own spiritual life seem like an obscene and selfish indulgence.

I suppose that most of us come to religion initially out of a sense of need, wanting the security of something that seems unchangeable. There is nothing unusual in that. But it seemed strange to me then, and still does, that religion is so often used to encourage dependency rather than to help people to grow up and stand on their own feet. No doubt a nurturing and neighbourly God accepted my intention to be a holy woman in the way that loving parents receive with amused delight the fistful of wilted flowers brought to them in the hot, grubby hands of their children or the unsuitable, garish Christmas gifts which will be lovingly displayed even if they cause aesthetic eyes to wince. There is no shame in having been a spiritual toddler.

In the post-Robinson era I began to reclaim the treasures I had relinquished when I became a deaconess. I wanted to be *human* rather than *holy*. I wanted a different kind of spirituality which would help me to grow up and take the risks of loving. I no longer wanted to live in a religious hothouse. You do not have to leave a religious order to do that of course and real religion does not encourage the kind of evasions I have written about. I did not consider leaving the Deaconess Order at that point, or for another sixteen years.

The change of direction was an inward one to begin with. I was beginning to think about a new kind of secular ministry—closer to the French worker priest model. I asked for a sabbatical year in which to think and pray, paint and write and consider possible ways of preparing myself for a new kind of ministry. When I describe it as 'new' I mean that until then it had never been an option in the Order to which

I belonged. Later a number of deaconesses moved out of church-centred work to become involved in various kinds of teaching and social work.

It was at this point in my life that I went to a retreat in North Yorkshire and met the person who was to be my companion in the new life I was moving into. She was already halfway through a course in social work training at Southampton University, not initially with a view to working in a non-church setting, but chiefly because she had felt ill-equipped to deal with the complex human problems which beseiged her in her work as a deaconess in a large housing estate in Basingstoke.

When we eventually chose to have a home together I do not think it ever occurred to me that we were doing anything unusual. There were those who thought we were. We belonged to an order in which there was a lot of pious nonsense talked about the danger of close relationships. We were encouraged to view them as temptations to be avoided since they might draw us away from our singular devotion to God. Long before *Honest to God* had encouraged us to revise the unhealthy bias of monastic spirituality I had rejected this as an affront to the experiment in costly friendship which Jesus began.

I do not think it occurred to either of us to resign from the Deaconess Order, though I am sure there were those who thought we should. We were aware that we had broken a taboo and it seemed important to stay and demonstrate how unwholesome that particular taboo had been. We did it without any banners or headlines, without making an issue of it. We did not think of ourselves as women of the new age, determined to take responsibility for our own lives and live in holy obedience to our inner wisdom. But I suppose that was what we had done, at a time and place in which there was no feminist movement within the British Churches to encourage or support us.

Now, in the last decade of this century I would like to think of myself as an enlightened woman with enough courage to live the truth that is in me. I want to learn how to be faithful to God by being obedient to the inner necessity of my life and the gifts I have been given.

Chapter 5
My Own Woman

I AM SHE
I will dance
To the edge of my time.

Will I rise dancing
When I reach that line
Or sinking fall?

No matter . . .
The dance is ALL.[1]

Quaker Women's Group, *I hope so* (poetry)

Since I gave myself to the service of Love.
Winning or losing,
I am resolved:
I shall give thanks at all times,
Winning or losing,
I shall live under her power.[2]

Hadewijch of Brabant (13th Century)

*Have there been moments in my life when I knew beyond question
who I was, and was able to affirm everything that I AM without
denial or evasion, without needing to justify myself? Is it only the
Son of God who can say 'I AM' with that kind of confidence?*
*Have I ever, I wonder, been completely and truthfully my own
woman, a woman after my own heart? Was there ever a time when
I refused to allow others to define the world for me?*
*Have I sometimes moved in a profound response to the inner law of
my own being and found the Will of God written there in the gift
that I am, in the things that delight me most, in the deep inward
necessity of my heart?*
Was there ever a time when I was not divided against myself?

I am not sure that I know how to answer this woman of a

42

new age who questions me so persistently. I know there-
have been times when I stepped clear of my conditioning
and said with my life 'I will be my own woman. I will walk
in the light of my inner truth. I will not be defined.' In this
book I explore some of the moments of liberation. But to put
it as I have done, as deliberate, self-conscious affirmation,
is really misleading. They were, in fact, times of revelation
when I forgot the narrow boundaries of my own selfhood
and found myself related to everything in the universe,
including myself. Or, they were moments when, like Eze-
kiel, I understood that love does not require us to grovel.

To talk about revelations or 'openings' is one way of putting it. Sacred literature and the autobiographical reflections of the saints make it all sound very grand and remote.
My moments of awareness are generally quite ordinary
ones. It might be a moment when, like Jeremiah, I am
pulled out of wintry depression by the sight of a tree in blossom or find myself astonished into worship by the play of
light on leaves. It might happen in a crowded tube at rush
hour when I see a small child and her West Indian father sitting hand in hand, beaming at one another, with love flow-
ing between them like a river of light. When I look back on
those transfigured moments, and others like them, they
have all been about the recognition of relationships.

*   *   *

The truth is that I cannot answer this new age woman I am
becoming who demands to know whether I am really my
own woman. I am not even sure whether her questions are
the right ones to be asking. All that I do know, as I look back
over the strange blessings and harvest of nearly sixty years,
is that I never wanted to be a conventional woman. I have
chosen to live without the fulfilments which were regarded
as so important to women of my generation. I have no
regrets about that. No doubt my choices were more restric-
ted than I knew but there were other options, other roads I
might have taken and chose not to take.

How did I become this woman who is such a strange mixture of confidence and anxiety? Is it any different from the

mix with which most of us have to live? Some of it is easily explained. The confidence I owe to the fact that I was a much-wanted and treasured first child. I seem to have spent a large part of my life working with, or listening to, those who know more about rejection and abuse than about being loved and wanted. Few of them ever had the confidence that I have when I come to a closed door and say 'this door will open for me.' It is a terrible bereavement, perhaps the worst there is, to enter a world in which no face looks back at yours with love.

The anxiety is more difficult to disentangle from the universal variety or the kind that accompanies us whenever we move into new or very stressful situations. Some of it is the legacy of having grown up in a home where there was very little money and from the fact that it was twice broken by bereavement by the time I was nine. But some of it stems from the same source as the inner confidence. There is a curious burden in being the much desired child of loving parents, the small inheritor of such huge hopes and expectations. The earliest, half subliminal message I can remember receiving was that much was expected of me.

It has taken me much longer than I expected to understand how sharply I have been defined by the next period of my life. Bereavement, guilt and grief were the main ingredients, but there were strange blessings in it too. I suspect that the long process of becoming my own woman began on a midsummer day in 1940 when a War Office telegram was delivered to our house. It brought my childhood world to an abrupt end. Bereaved children do not lose only one parent. The mother I had known vanished too, first into grief and then into the sheer necessity of being a breadwinner. As soon as I began to emerge from my own sense of shock and outrage I felt that our roles had been reversed and that I was now responsible for her.

Childhood bereavement is always devastating. It has its own curious compensations. I no longer expected other people to sustain me. I had to begin to sustain myself, withdrawing into my inner world, discovering my own resources for survival and learning how to live with the aloneness which belongs to us all. It was a double-edged blessing of course, for in the end I knew a lot about being independent and self-reliant but much less about trusting other people. I found my own thoughts more interesting and entertaining than those of other people. Learning to listen to others has been a much harder discipline for me to learn and being so inept about it has deprived me of some of the encouragement I needed.

*   *   *

My father was an unusual man. He was the odd one out in a large Cockney family. He left school at fourteen, unskilled, but determined to teach himself all that he wanted to know about the world. He was a Sunday painter and a passionate bibliophile. He was killed at Dunkirk when I was nine. I can remember very little about him, though I know all the important things. Some of my memories were blanked out by the trauma of his death which followed so swiftly on that of a younger sister. My grandparents, who lived with us, had never forgiven my mother for marrying, as they put it, 'beneath her.' Consequently he was never mentioned and what I might have learned from my mother was never spoken of until long after my grandparents had died.

When he died I inherited two things that told me much of what I needed to know about him. One was his small library; English literature, poetry, botany and travel books, history (particularly the history of art) were his chief delights. As I read them from cover to cover they became mine too. The other bit of my inheritance was a small black drawing book. I still have it. In it he recorded some of his own moments of vision. They were moments of awareness of what George Herbert calls *'heaven in ordinarie.'*[3] I know from the way my father drew the folds of an old coat on a peg, the curve of a woman's body, a long flank of down-land, a bird in flight or a small boat drawn up on a pebbled beach that he saw the world as I do, as a source of infinite wonder and endless fascination. From him, although he was out of sympathy with organised religion, I got the message that Life is a gift, and all its forms should be reverenced and respected.

My father's small collection of books opened a door for my escape into different worlds. I spent hours in ancient Rome or wandering round the Paris of the Impressionists. I knew the Bronte country almost better than the suburban sprawl of the expanded village in which we lived. Words began to fascinate me, and when I left school I spent hours in second-hand bookshops and came away with my arms full of sixpenny treasures.

I began to read psychology. It helped me to understand the burden of guilt and grief that I had been unable to share with anyone else. The books I read were written long before we began to understand the more subtle aspects of guilt in those who survive disasters. Two members of my family had died at an early age. I was alive and compelled to find a meaning in my survival. It gave an added seriousness to my search for a vocation.

*   *   *

When I hear radical feminists talking about a world ruined by men I find myself looking back to the gentle, sensitive man who left as his chief legacy to me, a love of the natural world, his passion for colour and form, his love of music and all the consolations of the world of books. He was humorous and loving. I can never remember him being discourteous. My mother occasionally smacked us for childish misdemeanours. My father was a natural Quaker. He detested all forms of violence, even the mildest slap or outburst of temper. On only two occasions can I recall him being angry. One was on the day when he had just completed a painting in oils and I drew a fascinated finger from top to bottom. The other occasion was when he found that I had decorated the end pages of one of his most treasured books with a series of drawings giving some evidence that I had discovered the anatomical differences between men and women. I was sent to bed on both occasions, but since he relented sufficiently to let me have a selection of books it became more of a luxury than a punishment.

I often wondered whether I had gilded his memory with all the lost goodness of my childhood world. But a few years ago when I was visiting my mother we found some of his last letters to her. As we read them together it was obvious that his sensitivity and gentle courtesy were not merely products of my nostalgic imagination. He was able to express tenderness in a way that is still difficult for many men. In spite of his lack of formal education he was able to express his thoughts and philosophical reflections more clearly than some university students who wrote to me when I worked for the Student Christian Movement. He had labelled himself an atheist and kept us from exposure to religious institutions but his wartime experiences had begun to disturb his religious indifference. He was beginning to explore the claims of Christianity. He was reading the New Testament for the first time. He wrote enthusiastically about all the new books he was reading and predicted confidently that the war was about to end and he would soon be with us again. I rate him as a rare and lovely human being, but not much of a prophet.

*   *   *

I know how terribly women have been hurt by the attitudes of men towards their insights and wisdom, their equal capacity for creative and rigorous thought. Perhaps I have lingered on the edge of the Women's Movement because my own experiences have been less painful. I have not been crushed, as some woman have, from the beginning. I have a sister, but no brothers with whom I was compared unfavourably in childhood. I have been privileged to enjoy ten years of higher education and to have worked in two professional fields.

I have never been unemployed, except voluntarily during my sabbatical year. I have not often felt that I was being discriminated against in a work situation and I have been singularly fortunate in the male colleagues with whom I have worked. I have never in adult life been economically dependent on a man. I have not been sexually or physically abused either in childhood or in adult life. The only sexual harassment I have known was at the hands of a much revered Methodist minister who seemed to believe that all celibate women must be aching for his embrace. I was slender in those days and able to run faster than he could. But in any case I have a withering look that has intimidated more men than have ever intimidated me.

I realise when I look back that my experiences have been very different from many women in the present phase of the feminist revolution. I grew up as an adolescent in war-time Britain, in a society in which women had to be inde-pendent and organise things for themselves. Occasionally men in uniform returned for brief intervals but it was women who ran the neighbourhood in which I grew up. I won a scholarship to a Girls' Grammar School. All my teachers were women.

If my mother's values and assumptions dominated and sometimes oppressed me it was from her that I learnt about courage and tenacity. Although we were desperately poor she was, and still is, a very warm and hospitable person, though she suffered, like many of her generation, from the taboo on tenderness. The only male chauvinist I knew was my maternal grandfather who lived with us and taught me the value of silence. He would have qualified for a star part in 'The Barretts of Wimpole Street'. In fact he and my grandmother managed to combine to a remarkable degree the less edifying aspects of Dickensian characters. In retro-spect I can see that they were two deeply unhappy people who projected onto us their terrible disappointment with life.

*   *   *

Apart from the experience of growing up in a household which, during my adolescent years, was dominated by a man who might well have qualified for an Olympic gold medal for chauvinism, I have not been as damaged as some women. It may be that I am fooling myself and am still not fully aware of the real extent of my oppression. But from my present viewing point I can see that some of the circum-stances which might have crushed me were the ones which made me inwardly self-reliant and fiercely determined to be my own woman and live my own life. No doubt some analysts would say that I did no such thing, and that having found human beings unreliable (even the most sympathetic being is likely to desert you by dying) I simply went for religion in a big way because it stood for something solid and enduring.

There is some truth in that of course and I am grateful that the first church I knew gave me an experience of Christian community. There were people in it who really cared for the fatherless stranger who had suddenly come among them. They saw promise and possibilities in me at a time when I was too shaken to see them for myself. Whatever problems I had later with Christian doctrines and other-worldly spirituality my first experience of the church was a positive one. I was loved into the kingdom/queendom by ordinary Christians who were probably not sophisticated enough to know the difference between orthodoxy and heresy, but they knew enough about loving to make me feel at home with them. They trusted me with responsibility and equipped me for it in a way that helped me to grow. I have valued the church not because it symbolised immutable truth but because I knew it first as a community of human beings who were learning to love one another and encouraging one another to change and grow.

The church as anything other than a community of the friends of Jesus has always been a problem to me. It was a problem to me long before feminist writers made us sharply aware of its patriarchal structures. Looking back at some of the influences in my life I found myself turning the pages of J. H. Oldham's *Life is Commitment*. It meant a lot to me when I first read it in 1953. I had been a church member for only four years but I found that I had underlined in red a conversation with Paul Tillich in which Oldham remembered saying 'You know, Tillich, Christianity has no meaning for me whatsoever apart from the Church, but I sometimes feel as though the Church as it actually exists is the source of all my doubts and difficulties.'[4]

Another important influence in my life at that time was

the writing and the broadcasts of C. S. Lewis. His avuncular voice was as well known to radio listeners then as Rabbi Lionel Blue's is today. The month before I left home for the first time, to work in a branch of the National Children's Home in Horsham, I went out and bought eight of his books to take with me. I loved *The Screwtape Letters* and *The Great Divorce*. When I was responsible for taking morning assemblies in a special school I serialised the chronicles of Narnia. They touched a deep nerve of longing in children who were labelled 'maladjusted' and slow-learning. To my surprise children who had regarded reading as a terrible chore and bore began to borrow the Narnia books.

C. S. Lewis was such a persuasive apologist, a good writer and a marvellous story teller that it was a long time before I realised how deeply his view of Christianity, which was one of the first I encountered, was coloured by his work as a medievalist. His fear of women, his ambivalence about sexuality, his inclinations to sado-masochism and all the dualisms of the medieval world view were powerful reinforcements to one another and no doubt served to reinforce my own pathologies. In spite of the debt I owe to him for making Christianity credible he was one of the first twentieth-century Christian apologists who encouraged me to undervalue the earth-loving spirituality that is more natural to me than most of the medieval models.

I began to write this chapter on the first Sunday in Advent. I finished it two days after the release of Nelson Mandela. During the period when I worked on it liberation movements began to break out all over eastern Europe. As I lit my Advent candle I was listening to Barbara C. Harris, Suffragan Bishop of Massachussets, preaching in the Cathedral church in Boston. When I lit the last of them the words of the *Magnificat* had taken on a terrible significance in an unofficial courtroom in Roumania.

George Fox was a passionate defender of the ministry of women but he would probably have looked askance at my Advent candles. Some Friends continue to hold a testimony against special times and seasons. Obviously I am not one of them. I might have been in the seventeenth century when early Friends voted with their feet and walked away from a church which seemed to have forgotten its prophetic and liberating ministry. As a new religious group they had such a vivid sense of God with them, within them, that they felt no need of any ritual or symbolic reminders of it. As many women do today they associated the rituals with their sense of oppression within the church and walked away from it to find the God within themselves.

I am still my own woman and not content with hand-me-downs or what is fashionable. I light my candles in Advent not because I dissent from our Quaker affirmation that all days are holy but because I cannot exclude the special holy days from the all. I know from my own experience that all places can be holy ground and all times and seasons full of advents and epiphanies, but I relish the special seasons of celebration too. I also think that George Fox got it wrong when he thought that we can live without ritual or symbols.

I light my candles partly because there is still a child in me who is capable of huge astonishment. I still catch my breath in wonder at the sight of candles burning in the darkness on a winter night. They touch something deep within me that I suspect will always prompt human beings to light candles in a dark time, for hope and for remembrance. I can still be overwhelmed at the sight of a tree full of light whether in high summer on an alpine slope, in spring or autumn in Sussex beechwoods or on Victoria station with the Salvation Army singing carols round it. Orthodox Quakers or radical feminists may smile regretfully at my lack of sophistication or proper understanding but I cannot afford to lose touch with the child within me. It is the part of me that is still playful and creative enough to make me into a woman of God's new age.

Chapter 6
Moments of Awareness

The flame of the first blade
Is an angel piercing through the earth to sing
God is everything
The grass within the grass, the angel in the
angel, flame
Within the flame, and He is the green shade
that came
To the heart of shade.[1]

Edith Sitwell, *How many Heavens . . .*

When we open ourselves to the ground of our
being this is an opening not just to the ground
of the self but also to God. In that self-opening
we discover who He is. The name of who He is
is love.[2]

Melvyn Matthews, *The Hidden Journey*

As you leave Eden behind you, remember your
home,
For as you remember back into your own being
You will not be alone.[3]

Kathleen Raine, *Collected Poems*

There are some things I have always known though it has
taken me over half a lifetime to recollect them. Some of
them I know intellectually but I knew them long ago at a
much deeper level. I know, for example, that in the womb
we recapitulate the evolutionary drama of the universe.
Every cell of our bodies carries within it elements of that
primal explosion of energy which brought our world into
being. We are children of the stars and know it in our blood
and bones as well as in our minds.

I know that I live in a dynamic universe which is a vast
web of interconnections so intimately related that economic
policies pursued in one hemisphere can damage our global

network beyond repair. Our genes contain the memory of our origins and our human choices affect the future of the cosmos, and perhaps whole worlds beyond our own planetary system. What this knowing does to my understanding of life and death I am still struggling to understand. It places a question mark for me over any kind of exclusive or other-worldly spirituality.

Children, poets, artists, mystics and women are perhaps more familiar with the kind of knowing that goes beyond the limitations of the rational mind and explodes our linear models of reality. I was three years old when I stood, like Eve in Eden, in my field of bright grasses and knew that I was a child of light. I knew, as George Fox did, 'the nature of things and virtues.'[4] I knew I was intimately connected with everything in the universe and always would be.

And then a cloud came and hid that bright transfigured world from my sight but left me with a memory of what I had seen and known. I suspect that many of us can recall experiences of wonder and inward knowing. They are part of what Edward Robinson defines as the original or primal visions of childhood, and that makes them very important for those who are learners and unlearners in the school of Christ.

Years later, when I first read Edith Sitwell's poem 'How Many Heavens' with its marvellous first line 'The emeralds are singing on the grasses . . . ' it stirred that memory of childhood and restored some of its meaning to me. Walt Whitman's 'Leaves of Grass' nudged me into another bit of recollection. I began to understand why I only had to see sunlight on grass to find myself stunned into pure amazement or bursting into inward *doxologies* or *glorias*.

The process of beginning to discover what we already know deep on the inside of our lives is one that takes us on a mystery tour of our own life experiences. Sometimes we find ourselves having to run the film backwards to recollect our earlier experiences. Sometimes our inward knowing may project us forward in time, as when we meet someone we know will be important to us or find ourselves understanding which part of our lives is due for further expansion. Many people can recount experiences of knowing that are quite explicit in terms of future events.

Sometimes a moment of vision may be a flash-point of discovery, a sudden illumination. Quite often it is a process of becoming aware of what we already know at some deep level in our lives. I recovered my childhood experience of being at home in the universe by a process of picking up clues and beginning to see the real significance of things that had been puzzling to me.

Long before I read Edith Sitwell's poem I had been pre-occupied with grass as a personal symbol of new life or being reborn. It kept appearing in my paintings during my sabbatical year. During that year I met Marion Milner, a Jungian psycho-analyst who used free drawing, what we would now call 'right brain' drawing, as a way of learning and self-discovery. She invited me to go to some of her creative painting classes in which she encouraged people to daydream with a paint brush and see what emerged.

In our flat in Bradford I began to experiment with this kind of free painting and found myself painting pathways through tall grasses with light streaming from a small clearing at the end of the path. I kept painting variations on the same theme. The first time I sat down and painted this long tunnel of light surging through what looked like a tall forest of grasses I found myself weeping. I couldn't understand why. It was not a very good painting but weeping over it seemed a bit excessive! It moved me so deeply that I was puzzled and rather frightened.

A few days after I had painted it Werner and Lotte Pelz came to stay with us. I had met them at an SCM Conference and invited them to visit us in Bradford. We talked about my plans to try and get into a College of Art. Neither of them thought it was a good idea. 'It will ruin your painting' they exclaimed with some passion. I wasn't sure whether it was me or the paintings that were on the verge of disaster, so I told them about my distress on finishing the first painting of light and grasses. 'Of course,' said Werner, 'Of course, it is obviously a "birth painting".' At that particular time in my life I was feeling very much as if my life had been turned inside out and I was moving into a new world. I accepted this diagnosis with a sigh of relief. It seemed to fit what was happening inside me.

It was even more disconcerting when another friend came to visit us and happened to be sitting in front of one of my paintings. To our astonishment she started to get very agitated and suddenly burst out 'I can't get through, I feel as though I'm choking.' She was a stocky, down-to-earth Lancashire woman and we were quite astounded for a moment at this quite uncharacteristic outburst. 'Was your birth a very difficult one?' I found myself asking. She looked surprised but admitted that her birth had in fact been a very prolonged and difficult one.

Even at that point I was puzzled as to why my tunnel of vivid grass should be a symbol of the birth canal. I still had no memory of the moment when I had stood, a toddler in Eden, and had known myself as a child of light.

At another crisis point I wrote a cycle of poems about grass. They were not about the shock of light which accompanies our birth experiences, and which those who have died, and been resuscitated, tell us is also part of the death experience. It was obvious to me later that they were poems in which I somehow incorporated my early experience into a system in which grass had become a personal symbol, which nourished me in difficult times as well as in moments of elation.

I called the first of these poems 'Grass on Rock'.

> Grass
> gripping the edges of this rock
> tenaciously
> as my green spirit
> obstinate and quiet
> clings to the gritty surface
> of its dream.
>
> Earth
> spins: shock and fracture
> of rock and dream
> will not dislodge this gleam

green flickering of hope
from its accustomed ledge
in wind and sun.

I went on picking up clues from the things that moved me most deeply. When I became an art student I discovered Van Gogh's *Ripening Corn* and *Meadows with Butterflies*. I read everything I could lay my hands on about this strange, sad visionary who painted grass as I saw it, ecstatic and tenacious, luminous and utterly down-to-earth. I discovered how often grass was a symbol of pulsating life to him; from his early paintings of allotments in Montmartre to his last two canvasses of vast fields of wheat blazing under dark and terrible skies.

I was an art student during the sixties when many students were experimenting with LSD and other drugs. I declined the invitation of some of my friends to take a 'trip' with them and be blown out of my mind. 'I can get high on grass, or blown out of my mind any time,' I said 'and it doesn't cost me a thing.' I was wrong of course. Visionary experiences have a terrible cost attached to them. To be sensitised by the Holy Spirit, or really open to the Spirit, in a way which transfigures the world and enables us to see it with new eyes, inevitably involves an equal sensitivity to the darkness and tragedy of human life. You can't have one without the other. There is no consciousness without pain, and total awareness is a crucial, sometimes crucifying business. How could it be otherwise? When William Penn wrote *No Cross, No Crown* he was using the language of the *Apocalypse* to say the same thing, though I don't believe it is simply a matter of sequence or linear progression from Calvary to Easter Morning. It can be the other way round as well.

Visionaries, who live more intensely our ordinary human experiences of heaven and hell, are never very far from the edge of darkness or depression. Awareness must obviously be of both the dark and light of human experience. The wilderness of self-doubt follows hard on the heels of Jesus' blinding moment of self-awareness by the Jordan. George

Fox's moment of ecstasy as he walked towards the prison in Coventry and felt himself 'ravished with the sense of the love of God'[5] is followed by the moment as he went into the prison when he felt the terrible power of darkness almost, but not quite, overwhelming him.

I can remember an occasion when, as a very young and inexperienced deaconess, I went to visit a bereaved family in the northern industrial village where I lived. The family were very poor. They were not church-goers, and had a reputation for being rough and tough. I cannot remember any of the details now but I do remember that as I turned the corner of the road in which they lived I was over-whelmed with a sense of the presence of God. It wasn't so much a sense of being ravished; I doubt if I would have appreciated that. It was more like being given a massive injection of peace and being held in that peace as I went in to be with the devastated family.

I am not suggesting that there is anything unusual in that experience. I have written about it for two reasons. The first is that we do ourselves a grave disservice if we elevate the experience of someone like George Fox so much that we put it in a class of its own. The sense of being strengthened inwardly or held in the light or love of God, either before or during a time of crisis is not at all unusual. My second reason for being anecdotal rather than discursive is to remind us that we know far more than we think we do.

Quite often I have talked about some particular experience of being inwardly reinforced and held in the peace and power of God, and the person with whom I have shared this will say, suddenly and awkwardly, 'I haven't told anyone this but I remember a similar experience when . . . ' I wonder why we deprive one another of hope by being so reticent about telling what we know of inward empowerment.

Sometimes our moments of vision or awareness seem to be given for no apparent reason at all. They are simply gratuitous, part of the business of being beneficiaries of what Peter described as 'the many coloured grace of God.'[6] C. S. Lewis wrote a poem to which he gave the title 'Day with a White Mark.' He described it as a very ordinary sort of day, in fact a day when vexations of all kinds threatened to disturb his equilibrium. Yet in spite of it all he found himself 'tossed and whirled in a preposterous happiness.' Reason told him his mood was unreasonable;

> Yet I—I could have kissed the very scullery taps, the colour of my day was like a peacock's chest . . .

With a good deal of wisdom he recognised that there is something quite unpredictable about days like that.

> Who knows if it will ever come
> again, now the day closes?
> No one can give me, or take away
> that key. All depends
> On the elf, the bird or the angel.
> I doubt if the angel himself
> Is free to choose when sudden heaven
> In man begins or ends.[7]

I can still remember quite vividly one of my days with a white mark. We were in the midst of the traumatic business of having just moved house. I was still in Leeds trying to complete some research. Our new house in South Wales was a ramshackle cottage which needed so much doing to it that our hearts sank whenever we looked at it. We closed the door on it and went for a walk instead. We walked for miles along the cliffs at Llantwit Major. It had been a late Spring but when it arrived it was like the first morning in Eden. This day was part of it. The sun shone. The sea was an incredible blue. The grass was fresh and vivid with resurrection. We came across a field full of cowslips, which we never saw again. The cliffs were covered with clumps of thrift. A woodpecker flew out from under a cliff. We came to a small valley running down to the sea, brilliant with spikes of early purple orchid.

And quite suddenly I was lifted out of myself and my

gloomy preoccupations with unfinished research and the business of living away from home. All that day I walked in a transfigured universe, in which there was no sense of being separate from it, or out of harmony with it. I was purely and simply happy, though it was only in retrospect that I realised it. At the time I was not *self* conscious at all. I was back in my field of bright grasses, with light pouring from every tree and blade of grass, and myself walking in the light.

*   *   *

Sometimes those days when the earth gives us its blessing come at precisely the moment when the blessing seems to have been taken away. They come at time of loss and uncertainty when it might seem that we have no reason for thankfulness at all. A few years ago I went to visit my doctor because of a rather frightening and violent pain quite unlike anything I had ever known. Our GP is an ex-army doctor who doesn't believe in wrapping things up. 'We'll investigate the worst possibilities first' he said and proceeded to make the necessary arrangement for me to go into hospital. It all happened so quickly that I was sure there must be something very seriously wrong. And it was all too obvious that he thought so too.

I walked out of his surgery feeling stunned, but not, as the books suggest, disbelieving. It seemed all too likely. Most of my life I'd done things in a rather excessive way. I took on more than I could cope with, I thrived, or thought I thrived, on huge challenges. There wasn't much about me that was sensible or moderate. I didn't feel angry or want to ask 'Why me?' And I wasn't out of touch with my real feelings either. I was frightened, regretful and sad.

Yet I walked out into the street and it shone like the New Jerusalem. I remember walking into town to get a prescription from the chemist. Houses, shops, pavements, bare winter trees, were all incredibly beautiful to me that morning. Everything was transfigured. Even the fishmonger's smile, when he handed us two cod fillets, seemed beautiful and very precious, as if it was a gift. In fact everything seemed to be an astonishing gift on that bleak morning when I wondered whether I was being asked to give it all back again.

When I came out of hospital after some very minor surgery I hoped I would be able to hold onto that vivid sense that life is a gift. But I didn't. It was a moment of vision given for a particular time. On bleak wintery mornings when I wake, sluggish and inclined to depression I still have to rehearse my lines and tell my drooping spirits rather firmly:

> This is the day that the Lord has made. I *will* rejoice and be glad in it.[8]

Chapter 7
Heart Work

Work of sight is done
now do heart work
on the pictures within you.[1]
Rainer Maria Rilke, *Letters of Rainer Maria Rilke*

One must disintegrate gladly, for God's holy
undoing of us to take place.[2]
Damaris Parker Rhodes,
　　　Truth: a Path and not a Possession

Divine gifts sound nice and easy, but as often
as not they are hard to take. They occur as
shocks, minor or major . . . For us to 'see ourselves as others see us' is always a jolting
experience, and more usually comic than
tragic.[3]

John Drury, *The Burning Bush*

The crisis which finally brought me into the Society of
Friends was a very ordinary one. Later I rationalised it and
dressed it up in all kinds of theological finery. There were
fragments of truth in that too. I needed to be part of a faith
community which names the whole of life as sacramental,
including the dark and difficult bits. I wanted space and
silence in worship. And, at that point in time, I was
troubled that there was an increasing dissonance between
the way in which past generations had expressed their faith
and my own experiences which seemed to be so different. It
did not occur to me that I was actually re-enacting the Biblical drama in my own personal mythology, though it will
become clear that I was. I thought that I could end the dissonance by joining a religious Society in which silence had
priority, credal affirmations were not required and the
canon of scripture was not a closed one.

The precipitating factor in the end was an ordinary

human experience of betrayal, a betrayal of so much that seemed important to me in human relationships. For some strange reason I was shocked to find myself capable of that kind of trust-breaking. I must have been extraordinarily arrogant or locked in some kind of innocence, to have been so irrationally surprised at my fall.

For a long time afterwards I gave myself a very bad time. For nearly thirty years I had been preaching to others about forgiveness and acceptance. I saw it as the crucial difference between real love and its compulsive counterfeits. But when it came to the crunch, I could not accept it for myself. I found it almost impossible to forgive myself for hurting two people very badly. I should say three, because I was hurting too. And I couldn't forgive myself for being a perfectly ordinary kind of sinner.

Looking back I know that Mother Julian was right in her understanding of sin as 'behovely' or necessary. I wonder what else would have brought me to my senses, or what else would have exploded my quite unrealistic self-image. I had seen myself as a loving, open and very honest person and a bit superior spiritually. In the delicious and suspended state of unreality in which lovers are invariably cocooned, I even saw my betrayal as rather splendid and noble. As Jeremiah observed, reflecting on the general hypocrisy of his own community, human beings are into the top grade when it comes to self-deception.

It was Jung's understanding of the 'shadow' that helped me, in the beginning, to understand this sudden exposure of the dark side of myself, though Freud would have had a field day too when it came to exploring all the things I had managed to lock away in my personal underworld. I had tried to be spiritual and self-sacrificing to the point of absurdity. I had ignored many of my own needs. Women in particular are very vulnerable at this point. We have been so successfully conditioned socially and religiously to be dispensers of comfort and aid to everyone but ourselves. I had tried to live in my head and my spirit and ignore the rest of my life. I had treated my body and my emotions as if they were unimportant appendages. Plato, and Augustine (and

62

his Mum!), had helped me to produce my own private version of hell and it was no wonder that all I had refused to acknowledge in myself had broken out with such savage efficiency.

It was time for me to get wise to the kind of person I was in reality rather than in my spiritual and intellectual fantasies. But I did not disintegrate gladly as Damaris Parker-Rhodes suggests that we should. In fact I wonder if there are any human beings who take kindly to seeing their comfortable self-image blown to bits. It took me nearly three years to begin to pick up the pieces or see the process as any kind of holy undoing.

My bookshelves are bulging with books on spirituality; Christian, Sufi, Buddhist, Hindu, Jewish and all the New Age versions. They squat there on my shelves like Heinz 57 varieties. During the crisis in which my comfortable, taken-for-granted self-image was exploded into fragments I found very little help in any of them. Perhaps I was not in any state to read them. Most of them seemed, at that time, to make diagnoses and prescribe treatment that was unhelpful and irrelevant. The Christian varieties seemed to be framed in a pre-Robinson era. I did not feel that I had deeply offended a God 'out there'. I knew that I had hurt and offended myself as well as the two people I cared about. I figured that if God were as loving as the Church claimed, he or she would be down in the dust with me, helping me to put my broken life together again, enabling me to understand, like Perceval in the legends of the Grail, that good and evil interlock within us all.

Julian of Norwich still spoke to me with her calm assurance that sin is somehow a necessary ingredient in our learning but that ultimately 'all shall be well, and all manner of things shall be well'.[4] I clung to that assurance like a drowning person. But I knew that her *Revelations* were the fruit of her own desperate internal struggle to hold on to her feminine insights and her stubborn refusal to accept that the sin-sodden liturgies and doom paintings of the medieval church had got it right.

If we are fortunate, as I was, there may be a crisis so devastating to us personally that only a kind of dying to the past and beginning again can enable us to make sense of the experience and learn from it. That sounds rather dramatic. On the surface I was coping successfully with a difficult and demanding job. I was respected as a spiritual leader in the church to which I belonged. I had a loving relationship. But my inner life was disintegrating, or at least *apparently* falling apart, and I knew it.

Ouspensky, a disciple of Gurdjieff, helped me at that time to understand that human beings are still in a state of evolution and that we are not only 'unfinished' and therefore capable of further evolution, but that we spend a great deal of our lives 'asleep' and unaware of it. I could have read the same thing in the advice of the writer of the first Johanine epistle — 'and it doth not yet appear what we shall be.'[5] but the heavy moralising of the Church got in the way, powerfully reinforced by my own perfectionism and self-oppression. I knew that I had been so lacking in self-awareness, so 'asleep' in terms of what was really happening, that my unawareness had caused a lot of pain to others as well as myself. Perhaps we all learned something of value from what had happened, but for me the important things wrested from it were a determination to stay in touch with myself, to learn from my own story and to grow as fast as I could in self-awareness. It may be that self-awareness is not quite the right term, but awareness is. I wanted to be sufficiently sensitive to what was going on in my inner life that I could begin to develop the kind of spirituality that would enable me to face reality rather than running away from it.

The crisis made me very sharply aware of how much the Church has encouraged dependency on the one hand, and on the other has expected too much of priests, ministers and professional religious who are supposed to be the official couriers where tours of God-country are concerned. It also made me much more aware, not only of my own neurosis, but of how many of our human hangups, our refusals to face reality, the temptation to have power over others, our lack of self-knowing, are all reflected in, and sometimes reinforced by the religious institutions to which we belong.

We try to invest them with an authority they do not have
and forget that like us they are a mix of grubbiness and
glory, good and evil, awareness and unreality.

It was Krishnamurti who, at that point, helped me most.
He helped me to discover a way of meditation which
looked, without trying to judge or blame, at what was happening in my life and at some of my illusions and unrealistic
expectations. What he had to say about listening and being
inwardly attentive was what I needed to learn. I could have
learned it from the Christian mystics but the traditional
God language seemed to get in the way and made it difficult
for me to hear what they were saying. I needed to come
away from all of that and find a space in which to learn how
to listen to myself and the God within me. I could not do
that in forms of worship that were cluttered with words and
crammed with assumptions about God that I could no
longer make.

It was during this period of unrest and longing for a way
of worship that would give me that kind of space, that we
went to stay with a friend who had recently become a member of the Society. She knew nothing of my emotional crisis.
I have no memory that we said very much about her
migration from Methodism to the Quaker way. We may
have talked about our difficulties with religious language or
sentimental and sanctimonious hymns. All that I do
remember is that she lent me two Swathmore Lectures.
One was Damaris Parker-Rhodes' *Truth—a Path and not a
Possession*. The other was Ralph Hetherington's *The Sense of
Glory*. Both of them articulated things I had been groping
towards or had already discovered. They were free of the
kind of religious language and concepts that I found so difficult. As Friends would say, they 'spoke to my condition',
and served to give me the final push which propelled me
away from my life as a professional religious.

Writing my letter of resignation from the Deaconness
Order, to which I had belonged for twenty-five years,
seemed to me one of the most painful and difficult things I
had ever done. It felt as if I was stripping off all the things
that had represented status and spiritual security. Looking

back, I am amused at the way in which I made such a high drama out of it all. It was much more like moving house or simply moving into a slightly larger room in which I had more space to move about and could breathe more freely. And in any case, I was already past the point of no return.

I have to admit that even in this larger space the air is sometimes musty with the odour of sanctity and heavy with assumptions about God and human beings that I no longer wish to make, simply because I live in the twentieth century, not the seventeenth in which the Quaker story began, or the first century in which the Christian story had its revolutionary beginnings. But who am I to talk about the reluctance of religious groups to change when it took me fifteen years and a major emotional crisis to come clean about myself and the inner changes that made my outward journey necessary.

I suppose it is never easy for human beings to admit their failures in living and loving, or to accept that they need help in understanding themselves. It is harder still for religious people to make that admission. I remember a senior social worker in one of the weekly workshops we ran in South Wales for training voluntary counsellors. He said on one occasion, 'This group is very important to me. At work I have to be seen as competent and capable of dealing with any and every crisis. This is the one group to which I belong in which I am able to talk about my weakness and failure'. He was also a faithful and regular attender of a church which is an interesting reflection on the difficulties that Christians have in being real with one another.

So many books on spirituality have pictured the Christian life as a journey from darkness to light, from sinful brokenness to some kind of shining perfection. Quaker spirituality has emphasised the business of walking in the light and given too little attention to an acceptance of the darkness within. Programmes of religious education have sometimes given misleading information on the subject of human beings in relation to God, talking about the sinfulness of the former and the holiness of the latter in a way that makes nonsense of the deepest insights in the biblical tradition. I am always amazed when biblical dogmatists or 'evangelicals' rest their case for mission on the idea that there are human beings somewhere on this planet who are without God. They seem to me to be ignoring completely the tremendous affirmation of the Hebrew writer of Psalm 139, who wrote, long before the Gospels came to be written, but understood very well that there is no place in the universe which can ever be described as without God, least of all the hells we make for ourselves.

Strangest of all, as Julian of Norwich observed, even Christians find it hard to believe in the reality of God's unconditional love. They find it easier to visualise God as their accuser, prosecuting rather than defending them, passing sentence on them rather than pouring blessings on them. It seems all too easy for religious people to collect picture postcards of God which are more reminiscent of a chamber of horrors than a universe in which Love is the name of the energy that holds it all in being. Our pictures of God are often more to do with our earliest experiences of feeling guilty and not O.K. in the presence of authority figures; or they may be projections of our own self-hatred and the tyrannical demands of a perfectionist super-ego.

After the 'Gifts and Discoveries' study programme had begun, I discovered that there were Friends who felt guilty about spending time on their own spiritual needs. It seemed the depth of depravity to them that they should take time off from being God's Girl Guides or Boy Scouts in a needy world. Spending time in keeping a journal as a way of exploring their own life experiences seemed to be the height of self-indulgence and emotional luxury. Time spent in study seemed wrong if it did not have an immediate knock-on effect in enriching ministry or enhancing the life of the meeting.

I know from my own experience that a good deal of over-work in the church (and elsewhere) has to do with distorted images of God, and the Protestant work ethic, both of which make us feel guilty about being rather than doing, or relaxing in the presence of God rather than imposing on ourselves a life sentence of hard labour. When I first went to work in Friends House I found that many people over-worked to the point of absurdity, and that I had the kind of workload which seemed to demand a single-minded devotion to it and a studious neglect of my own needs or those of my family.

In fact, within three and a half years, I had come as close to burn-out as I have ever been. One or two Friends to whom I talked seemed to think that I ought to consider it a privilege to burn myself out in the service of Friends. Others had done so gladly. Why was I protesting? Eventually I found my way to a Jesuit spiritual director who asked me two important questions. The first was: 'How do you decide on your priorities?' and the second: 'What are your pictures of God?' The first helped me to sort out what aspects of the job were really important and within the scope of one person's capacity. The second helped me to understand that it was not God who was asking me to be a workaholic. Perhaps there is never more than a razor's edge between the giving away of our lives in love, as an act of freedom, and the uneasy servitude and self-sacrifice that is prompted by fear of what others will think if our diary is not impressively over-loaded or what God will do if we take time out to enjoy the world. I shall always be grateful to a Jesuit father for helping me to discover the difference.

I have lost a lot of illusions since I became a member of the Society of Friends. If, like me, you suffer from illusions a great deal, there is only one effective cure. You have to let go of them. I wish I could submit to this kind of relinquishment gracefully or at least with a certain amount of dignity. But, alas, I do it, as I do most things, the hard way, with a lot of sweating, huffing and puffing and grumbling about the discomfort.

I know it is not fashionable to talk about a personal God any more. Theologians mutter about anthropomorphism and sophisticated Friends look at you in a sympathetic but patronising way as if you are suffering from a complaint which they have managed to avoid through a careful diet of silence and image-free worship. I understand the diffi-culties, but I have to admit that I do a lot of this grumbling and complaining direct to the management. I have carried on this internal conversation with God for a long time now and it seems to be the only thing that has kept me free from ulcers or chronic resentment. The Hebrew poets who wrote the Psalms did a good deal of it too. Job did it and got a sublime and slightly snooty answer. Jeremiah did it with as much depressive moaning and groaning as I do, which means I am in good company, religiously speaking.

I always think of myself as having been a rather shy and unobstrusive child but I may have got it wrong. Apparently I was the only girl in our Junior School to get 'the strap'. I received several lashes of it for talking too much in class. With God too I have been garrulous. Learning how to use the silence in meeting for worship has helped me to listen more and begin to understand prayer much more in terms of the wordless communication of the heart.

One of my illusions was rather like Thomas Merton's illusion that becoming a Trappist monk would give him the space for contemplation that he needed. I thought of the Society of Friends as a religious group which gives high priority to the inward journey. This was partly because I came to know it first through the writing of three American Friends; Thomas Kelly, Rufus Jones and Douglas Steere all of whom give high priority to the mystical aspects of Quaker spirituality. I discovered their books in our College library when I was reading theology and training to be a deaconess. I was so impressed that I spent every College Quiet Day reflecting on them. I spoke of my admiration for them to one of my New Testament tutors. My memory is that she smiled rather ruefully and said: 'But they are not even Christian'. Her memory of the exchange is that she ventured to suggest that Quakers were rather poor on theology. She may be right. Memory is a strangely selective thing.

Another illusion I had was that Friends were intrepid explorers of inward space. Like many newcomers to the Society I was rather awed by all the Quaker jargon about 'centring down', 'being gathered', 'walking in the light' and so forth. It made a meeting for worship sound like a launching pad for spiritual space travellers. I assumed from all the books I read that Friends would be able to give me lots of help in going further on the inward journey. And of course some of them have. But I have been surprised at the number of Friends who are very uneasy and suspicious about what seems to them unhealthy introspection or spiritual self-indulgence. They are more concerned about mending the world than about allowing themselves space for healing the tears in their own psyche. Meeting for worship is simply the place in which they plug in their exhausted spiritual batteries for re-charging in order to get on with the more serious business of putting the world to rights.

I have a lot of sympathy with that point of view. There is a part of me that values the down to earthness of Quaker spirituality. I could write a book in defence of the kind of ethical mysticism that Friends have espoused. But there is another part of me, a wise old woman perhaps, who knows quite well that it is not a case of either/or. The inward journey is as important as the journey outward towards others. I am not sure that they can ever be separated. If we neglect to learn the balance between them we shall learn, as I did, the real cost of our evasion. What we are really uttering on the inside of our lives will burst out sooner or later and often in ways that disconcert both us and others.

I remember an occasion when I was staying in the Penn Club and was introduced one morning to two Friends who seemed to have worked in every continent, doing all kinds of relief work, beavering away to improve the quality of life for others. I had breakfast with them and by an oversight, the waiter, a young Spanish boy, failed to bring their bacon and eggs as swiftly as he had brought mine. Their annoyance erupted into an explosion of anger out of all proportion to the offence. I suspect that in all their busyness on behalf of others they had somehow failed to stay in touch with themselves. No doubt they had spent their lives dealing with the needs of starving people and underdeveloped countries and had failed to listen to the hungry child within themselves. They had neglected their own need for rest and refreshment to such an extent that a minor delay in the arrival of their breakfast had caused them to regress and behave like two thwarted toddlers stamping on the nursery floor.

If prayer is not something we do so much as listening to what is being prayed within us, the real crying of the heart before God, then those two Friends who had deprived themselves for the sake of others were praying in their anger: 'O God, we are so hungry too'.

For a moment, the Pharisee in me was tempted to preen itself and say smugly: 'Thank God I am not like that.' Then I remembered the way in which my own unacknowledged needs had caused much greater havoc than that, and that those who seem to us to be selfish and insensitive are generally those who have failed to be sensitive to their own deepest needs and have not yet learned to love themselves generously.

Attending to the real prayers that we are crying on the inside of our lives is part of the spiritual or inward journey. Discovering our own gifts is another. Learning to love the world in our hearts and to understand that we are not one but many selves is yet another aspect of it. In the end it is not simply a matter of discovering our potential for evil as well as good, or clearing away the debris of unfinished business. All real religion and all good fairy tales remind us that the purpose of our exploration is to find the treasure hidden within our own lives. It always seems to me that there is a profound sadness in those human beings who never risk the perils of the inward journey, a wistfulness that is never quite concealed no matter how holy or competent they may appear to others. 'What,' says Jesus, 'does it profit anyone, to gain the whole world if in the process they lose the treasure of their own selves.'[6]

Today the need to know ourselves, to explore the mystery of our hidden life, to befriend the dark as well as the light in us, has become a matter of life and death. Those of us who live in the post-holocaust, post-Hiroshima era can no longer deceive ourselves that evil will disappear when people are better fed, and housed, better educated, more rational or more devout. We have to get wise to ourselves and learn to love rather than reject the world within us. Otherwise we shall always need enemies on to whom we can project all that we cannot accept in ourselves. We know now that unless we do, it is likely that an upright, well-educated, affluent, church-going (possibly 'born again') member of the human race may press the button that extinguishes civilisation. It was Thomas Merton, Trappist monk extraordinary, who once said that: 'only the man who has fully attained his spiritual identity can live without the need to kill.'[7] I might want to re-phrase it: 'only the woman who can trust the holy within herself can live without the need to be destructive'.

There is nothing new about speaking of spirituality in terms of the metaphor of the inward journey. It belongs to the language of mysticism and contemplative prayer, but at another level it is only another way of talking about how we grow up and find out who we are. Whether we use religious or non-religious language to describe the human journey, it seems to involve shedding a lot of illusions on the way and learning to accept paradox and uncertainty as the stepping stones by which we negotiate the river within and cross from spiritual adolescence to maturity.

The way to discovering our real life is, as Jesus hinted, never easy. It is narrow and daunting enough to deter the faint-hearted. It involves saying 'no', not to our real selves, but to the ego that postures and parades and thinks itself rich and holy. It is never an easy thing for religious or wealthy people to do, not because religion or wealth are wrong, but because their possession protects us from life and from understanding our real needs. Awareness of inward impoverishment is the most likely point of departure for spiritual journeys. We start from not having, not knowing, not understanding and begin the difficult business of finding out who we are and what we really want at the deepest level of our lives.

I could have learned it in another way perhaps, but it has been chiefly through the insights of Jungian and humanistic psychology that I have learned the rudiments of self-awareness. I believe that kind of learning is a spiritual discipline and one which the church is beginning to reclaim. It has been in the silence of Quaker meetings as well as in daily periods of reflection, meditation and journal writing, that I have begun to explore my inner world with much more confidence and to do what Rilke called: 'heart work, on the pictures within.'

Chapter 8
Spirituality as Awareness

We can never attain to the full knowledge of
God until we have first known our own soul
thoroughly.[1]

Julian of Norwich, *Revelations of Divine Love.*

When I first came to religion I wanted to know
more about God because I was frightened of
knowing too much about myself. Lots of
people use piety to evade or avoid. But as the
kingdom of heaven is within you, you can't
know one without knowing the other, and if
you try it it produces some nasty results such
as fanaticism, holy wars and persecution. The
doubts we suppress inside ourselves become
the 'heretics' we suppress in the world
outside.[2]

Lionel Blue, *Bolts from the Blue.*

Many religious people never come to possess
their inner selves and use their forms of worship as a vaccination to keep them safe from
any living experience.[3]

Damaris Parker Rhodes, *Truth — a Path and not a
Possession.*

Even though it was the Master's Day of Silence a traveller
arrived and begged for a word of wisdom that would guide
him through life's journey.

The Master nodded affably, took a sheet of paper and
wrote a single word on it 'AWARENESS'.

The visitor was perplexed, 'That's too brief' he said,
'would you expand on it a bit?'

The Master took the paper back and wrote again —
'AWARENESS AWARENESS AWARENESS'.[4]

All the experiences I have tried to describe in this book have been about different kinds of awareness. Those which some might want to label as ecstatic, mystical or 'peak' experiences I prefer to call 'eye-openers' or what George Fox would have called 'openings'. They were simply moments when I was intensely aware of the Mystery in which we live and move and have our being. Generally they were moments when I was unselfconscious or when I knew at some deeper level of being that I was not a separate 'I' at all. Whatever that deeper level of consciousness was it did not begin or end in me. It was somehow part of the 'eternal now' of being.

Twentieth-century writers have drawn such vivid pictures of our alienation that we have almost believed that we *are* separate individuals trapped in the prison of our own skin. There are times when we know this is not true. We listen to music or make love, we care deeply for other human beings, create something good and beautiful, work for some cause that is important to us, meet in worship: and the prison gates of our separate selfhood fly open without our having noticed. Love and wonder spring the latch continually.

Moments of knowing make nonsense of our western concept of individuality but they cannot deliver us from the need for another kind of knowing that is part of the discipline of love. When Meister Eckhart wrote 'No one can know God who has not first known himself'[5] he was reminding us of a paradox. Our real liberation from self-absorption lies on the other side of a journey in self-knowing. We *need* to know ourselves or the world will never be safe from our potential for exploitation and terrible destructiveness.

I have sometimes been sad and sometimes very angry when Friends have resisted and criticised any attempt to introduce the insights of humanistic psychology and self-awareness exercises into conferences, workshops or yearly meeting sessions. Even when we believe that they are not likely to be of much use to us we have no right to prevent others from learning.

Critics of self-awareness exercises have talked as if there

is something indecent, self-indulgent or morbidly intro-
spective about getting to know ourselves. I have been sad-
dened because we are one of the religious groups which
actually offers a real space for personal growth and exploring inner space. It seemed strange to hear Friends talking as
if all that mattered was putting the world right without pay-
ing any attention to our inner world and what is happening
there.

I have been angry because what looks like indulgence or
morbid introspection to some is in fact a path to integration
and liberation for those who have the courage to take it.
Nor is there anything new about the idea that self-knowing
and becoming aware of our potential is a way of knowing
God. Teresa of Avila pictured the self as a great castle con-
taining many rooms. Progress in the spiritual life involved a
disciplined exploration of all of them until the person concerned could arrive at the centre of the castle where God
was. In the *Gospel of St Thomas* Jesus says 'If you bring forth
what is within you, what you bring forth will save you. If
you do not bring forth what is within, what you do not
bring forth will destroy you.'[6] Mysticism is an important
strand in the evolution of the Quaker tradition and the
Christian mystics tell us that self-awareness is the necessary prelude to the knowledge of God.

The discovery that self-knowing is the way to God-knowing is not new. It is lodged in the mystical core of all
religions. What is new is the proliferation of all kinds of
groups concerned with the development of greater sensitivity and awareness. Most of them have come into existence since the end of World War II when the shock of
discovering what ancient civilisations and Christian
nations were capable of doing gave a cutting edge to the
need to know ourselves better.

They have flourished partly because churches have failed
to demonstrate effectively their relevance to the tensions
and creative possibilities of human living or to make it
abundantly clear that the Christian 'good news' is about the
liberation of our potential. There is very little in what the
writers of the gospels wanted to say about Jesus which sug-

gests that he would have approved of the oppressive and life-denying spirituality which has sometimes been promoted in his name. Nor has Christianity always been presented as a way of enabling us to become fully human and alive. It has been presented much more often as if its truth were settled long ago with no room left for development, fresh interpretations or new ways of discovering and imaging God. During the period of writing this book we have seen fresh outbreaks of hysteria and hostility when more courageous clerics have suggested that the system is open to new ways of understanding.

Of course religious freedom has its own peculiar dangers and anxieties. It contains, as life does, the possibility of making mistakes or even fatal errors. The Society of Friends is a religious group which values freedom. It holds in trust a way of worship which has always been something of a dangerous and daring experiment, though that may not be obvious to those of us who have experienced its weary predictabilities. It owes its existence to the originality and creative genius of George Fox, of whom it was said 'he was no man's copy.'[7]

Some of George Fox's spiritual insights sound very strange to us today, which is not particularly alarming for us because he did not suggest that there is anything fixed or final about religious belief. He reminded us that a living faith does not need to justify itself by quoting even the most sublime authorities. What *is* important is whether we know who we are and what it means to walk in the light of truth, whether we are able to speak out of our own experience of hearing the Word of God within us. We are, whether we are comfortable about it or not, members of a community of faith which trusts itself to the contemporary communication of the spirit and does not believe that God's last word was spoken in the closing verses of the *Book of Revelation*.

Our affirmations about our Christian roots and the beginning of the Quaker story are no more important to us than our willingness to say a holy 'yes' to the work of the spirit in us today. It is what our Friend Douglas Steere describes as 'being present where you are . . . '[8] not where the first century friends of Jesus were or even seventeenth-century Friends, but where we are today. It is very difficult to live in the present moment as Douglas Steere suggests. We spend a good deal of our time hindered by things that happened in the past, by unexamined assumptions and prejudice or being anxious about what may or will happen to us in the future. We are not one but many selves, and all of these things make it difficult for us to recognise the 'sacrament of the present moment'[9] and respond to it with all that we are.

We cannot be present *where* we are without the hard work of discovering *who* we are. There are some Friends who seem to believe that we ought to be more like early Friends, modelling our lives on George Fox or John Woolman as if our own uniqueness and originality were not precious gifts of God. Not surprisingly such Friends are disappointed because we do not measure up. Of course we do not and cannot. Our job is to be what we are. To be anything else is as sad and as silly as trying to be a photocopy of Jesus. There is an old Rabbinic story told by Rabbi Zusya about the last judgement in which he points out that when he arrives at the gate of heaven God will not ask 'Why were you not Moses?' or 'Why were you not Elijah?' but 'Why were you not Zusya?'

We are happy to affirm with George Fox that God is our contemporary inward tutor. We have a Query which asks ' . . . do you keep your mind open to new light from whatever quarter it may arise?' It seems strange, therefore, that we have been so reluctant to welcome what can be learned from the insights of depth psychology and the ways of self-understanding which have developed from them.

Some churches have welcomed these new ways of expanding human awareness and made extensive use of them in conferences, workshops and adult learning programmes. Catholic retreat houses run weekends on Psychosynthesis, spiritual and personal growth through Journal Writing, and Myers Briggs Workshops. Retreat programmes make use of self-awareness training in conjunction with Ignatian exercises and silent meditation. Courses for spiritual counsellors include self-discovery methods in their training programmes.

In Philadelphia Yearly Meeting, Pendle Hill Study Centre has given space in its learning programme to a wide variety of self-awareness workshops. In London Yearly Meeting we seem to have been much slower to respond to these opportunities to develop a better understanding of ourselves. Some aspects of the human potential movement have filtered into the Quaker system through workshops and conferences at Woodbrooke and Charney Manor, through the use of Q-Pac and the Quaker Networker projects, and in the training in conflict resolution developed by the Kingston Workshop. But many Friends remain aloof and suspicious of what they call 'gimmicks' or unhealthy introspection.

Some of the comments and criticisms about the introduction of self-awareness exercises into part of the 'Gifts and Discoveries' study programme were very amusing if they had not also been rather sad. Friends who were quite happy to quote John Woolman or Thomas Kelly at me observed suspiciously—'It is all very American isn't it?' Others have muttered darkly about half-baked psychology and morbid introspection.

I wonder where we got the idea that digging for the treasure hidden in our own lives, tracing our own story and clearing away obstacles to our excavations and self discovery is a form of morbid introspection? I can still remember the sadness in the voice of a Friend in one of our Monthly Meeting Residential Conferences when she was asked to make a list of things she liked about herself. She said at the end of the exercise 'I cannot think of a single thing I like about myself.' She was not alone in making that observation. It seems a sad reflection on the kind of spirituality which has made us specialists in the sin of dis-self-esteem. *That* is the kind of spiritual discipline which I would want to label *morbid*.

We need to become aware of what Elizabeth Kübler-Ross describes as the 'unfinished business' in our lives. Some years ago I used a slide/sound sequence at one of our Representative Councils. It was intended to illustrate the theme of continuing creation. I wrote a paraphrase of the Prologue of St John's Gospel to express our twentieth-century understanding of the origins of life. To my surprise one Friend objected to the sequence because he felt it had been too emotive and manipulative. His sharp reaction, as we later discovered, illustrated very clearly the need to deal with 'unfinished business' as well as our need to take responsibility for our own responses to situations which are difficult for us.

The Friend concerned could have said quite truthfully 'I did not like that presentation' or 'I found it rather disturbing.' He could have been critical of my selection of the material or the way it had been presented. It would have been quite proper to question the way I had chosen to re-translate a part of John's Gospel. Instead he wanted to challenge my integrity by labelling the sequence as manipulative. Whenever we are disturbed by our response to a particular situation, or over-react to something in a way that is inappropriate or out of all proportion to the event which triggered our reaction, we can be fairly certain that what we have done is project our feelings onto whatever or whoever has inadvertently been the trigger for our discomfort. I do it quite often when I find myself in any situation in which the fears and anxieties of my childhood experiences are re-activated.

Eventually the Friend at our Representative Council was able to look at his reaction and with the kind of honesty we value as Friends he began to unravel what lay behind it. He had a life-long distaste for John's Gospel which was partly an intellectual one but chiefly the result of the way which John 3:16 has been used by some evangelists as a kind of emotional blackmail to pressurise people into commitment. I had a lot of sympathy for him at that point and could understand how my visual meditation had reawakened old hurts and profound repugnance for the methods of some evangelists.

We need to develop awareness of our particular emotional reflexes, the points at which we wince or cringe and the circumstances which trigger off our sense of unease or anxiety. Awareness will not liberate us from them but it can defuse the explosiveness of our reactions and help us to take responsibility for them. It can also give us a clearer idea of where we need to work on our 'unfinished business' and be open to healing and rehabilitation.

The more I have thought about it the more I have become aware that some of our reluctance to learn more about our inner life comes from a bias within our own tradition. Friends have stressed the inwardness of religion and the work of the Spirit as inward teacher but we have developed this understanding in terms of a mysticism which is prophetic and strongly ethical in its outworking. Ignoring much that Friends like George Fox or John Woolman have told us about their own inner worlds we have concentrated on a holy obedience which has to do with changing the world around us. We have not been as much concerned about feelings or states of mind or experiences of ecstatic union with God as about the business of getting God's work done. We have valued the 'peak' experiences of Quaker mystics like Fox and Penington because they have been worked out in terms of a heightened sensitivity to human need and a desire to mend the world. Our bias has been a healthy 'so what' to ecstatic or altered states of consciousness unless they happen to produce the fruits of the Spirit in altered life styles and more conformity to the ethical imperatives of the Gospel. The bias is less healthy, I believe, if it leads to disregard for our own needs, a lack of compassion for ourselves or a loss of contact with what is happening on the inside of our lives.

It was Jung who, after a lifetime of counselling those who had neglected and oppressed themselves, wrote:

> That I feed the hungry, that I forgive an insult, that I love my enemy in the name of Christ—all these are undoubtedly great virtues. What I do unto the least of my brethren, that I do unto Christ. But what if I should discover that the least among them all, the poorest of all the beggars, the most impudent of all the offenders, the very enemy himself—that these

are all within me, and that I myself stand in
need of the alms of my own kindness—that I
myself am the enemy who must be loved—
what then?[10]

Jung goes on to suggest that at this critical point we
reverse our Christian attitude to offenders and those in
need, and rage against ourselves with a ruthlessness and
lack of pity we should be ashamed to demonstrate to
others. Instead we avoid the cry of our own beseeching and
cloak our poverty with still more busyness on behalf of
others. It gives us an air of superiority and virtue and a feeling of being in control which may deceive others and allows
us to go on deceiving ourselves.

There is a lot to be said for the rather austere way in
which Friends have regarded discipleship. It is refreshingly
unsentimental and free of spiritual gushing. Some of us
were drawn to the Society because of its 'no nonsense' attitude towards faith and praxis. But we have paid a high
price for this sturdy disregard for our own needs and our
failure to learn how to love the world in our own hearts. We
have deceived ourselves by imagining that doing God's
work does not include the heartwork of self-learning and
liberating ourselves.

I have counselled a number of people who were very
close to death and full of grief about it. It was not that they
were lacking in courage or terrified of the unknown though
both would be understandable. It was the fact of their own
unlived life that was causing them so much distress. As
they came close to death they were grieving because they
had never discovered their own destiny or lived to the full a
life that was truly theirs. Sometimes their feelings seemed
to be justified. They had gained a whole world of success or
wealth, their outward virtues had been applauded by
others but an inward sense of reality was insisting that
somehow they had gained it all at the cost of losing their
real selves. It is very painful to be with people as they grieve
for all the unrealised possibilities of their lives whatever our
own personal convictions may be about the limitless gener-

osity of God's grace or the Christian hope that the purposes of love cannot be thwarted by the apparent finality of death.

Sometimes what those who are dying feel about their lives is not justified. I can remember going to see Damaris Parker-Rhodes not long before she died. I owed so much to her. It had been her Swarthmore lecture that had given me the final push towards the Society of Friends. I knew her as a warm generous human being who had lived her life to the full. Yet towards the end of it she began to feel that she knew very little about loving. I understood what she meant. In learning to love ourselves and others we are always in the shallows of what is after all a vast and unfathomable ocean. We may splash in the shallows, wade in further and even swim out bravely until we are out of our depth but we shall never manage to navigate more than a small expanse of it.

But I remember her with thankfulness as a Friend who was never afraid to do heart work or to live experimentally. Death as well as Life was such an adventure to her that she sometimes failed to understand the feelings of those who were less at home with both. Her need to be honest to herself and speak out of her own experience were sometimes difficult for those who lacked her spiritual tenacity, but she reminded us always that 'the way out is the way in'[11] and, gave many of us the courage to go in deeper.

Towards the end of her life she also began to feel that Friends had paid too high a price in cutting themselves off from the healing rituals and symbols more familiar to those in the mainstream Christian tradition. I have often wondered whether she came to that conclusion partly because in our elected silence we find it hard to allow our own feelings of anger, guilt, grief or exaltation to find their expression. Celebration and lamentation are missing notes in our worship. We are often ill at ease when they do break in on our accustomed stillness.

When I was visiting Friends in America I was impressed at the way in which they were in the process of inventing new ways to enable one another to do heartwork and homework on themselves. They had created Meetings for healing damaged emotions, for healing the memory, meetings and conferences for the discovery of gifts and ministries — all as imaginative attempts to liberate Friends to be more fully and hopefully themselves. I wish that we could find similar ways to encourage one another to grow in awareness and understanding.

The inner journey, the business of digging to find treasure in our lives, does require courage. It is often lonely work and cannot be otherwise, but we could give each other much more support in doing it. There are times when we come upon parts of ourselves that are difficult to accept or when we find ourselves temporarily overwhelmed by some grief that we have never worked through or fully understood.

In my own experience and from a long and varied experience in pastoral counselling I have learned that each of us has an inner wisdom or what Rilke calls 'a guard within'[12] which protects us from what we are not yet able to face and allows us to know when we are strong enough to work on the buried material. All of us accumulate a good many griefs and losses in the course of our lives. For a variety of reasons we cannot always work through them when they occur. We live in a society which has deprived us of many of the rites of passage and grieving rituals which once enabled us to express grief and anger and allow them to pass away. Our obligations to the living may prevent us from doing our griefwork at the appropriate time and the longer we leave it the more difficult it is to cope with when it does overtake us.

Getting in touch with buried feelings is not morbid or unhealthy. Keeping the lid on them is. All the time we are not able to bring them into the light of our consciousness we are using vital energy to suppress our real feelings, and that energy is not available to us for living creatively. We are literally blocked or inhibited by our refusal to examine what is happening on the inside of our lives. We cannot open them up to the possibility of change and new life. Friends have particular difficulty at this point because they find it so hard to express anger and use it creatively. I have often wondered whether that is one of the reasons for the atmosphere of depression I have sensed in some meetings. Anger (or any strong feelings, which cannot find proper expression) is fertile soil for depression. If we dare not acknowledge our real feelings we cannot afford to feel anything at all, and if we cannot deal with conflict except by coating it with sweetness and light we lose the opportunity for real unity and peace.

One of the things I have noticed as I have visited meetings and read the evaluation papers of those who have completed the first phases of the 'Gifts and Discoveries' study programme is how often we feel intimidated by the pressures of a group or the 'authority' of the printed page. It is as if we do not trust our own perceptions of reality or value our own experiences sufficiently to respond without defensiveness to what others have said or written.

Instead of being able to say quietly in conversation with ourselves or others 'my own experience is different' or 'I have not found it helpful to think in those terms' we seem to get ourselves in a terrible lather either with the compilers of the course or with members of the group who express their faith differently or understand their life experiences in a quite different way. We seem to find it incredibly difficult to celebrate our differences or to listen to and learn from the experience of others.

One of the reasons for our difficulty arises from our openness in providing hospitality to large numbers of new Friends and Attenders who, like myself, have come to the Society from different religious traditions. Sometimes those who find their way to us have felt oppressed or damaged by their previous experiences of learning in religious groups. Part of their experience of hurt expresses itself in an over-reaction to those who use language or images of God which they have wanted to leave behind. I was very impressed by the way in which some Meetings in America had responded to this situation. I discovered that some of them do not accept Attenders into full membership until they have worked through their feelings of hurt and anger about the tradition from which they have come and know why it is they want to become part of the Society of Friends and what kind of spiritual authority *is* important to us. It is the kind of homework that some of us have to do before we can let go of unrealistic expectations about the Quaker way, or any compulsion to make its discipline and praxis conform to our illusions and dreams.

In London Yearly Meeting we seem to be rather timid about asking eager Attenders to wait until a period of adjustment has taken place and they are reasonably clear about what is on offer to them in the Quaker tradition and whether it is likely to meet their needs or approximate to their heartfelt hopes. We are afraid that they may feel even more hurt and rejected if we counsel them to wait. In the end I suspect there is much more hurt when we duck the issue.

I am not suggesting that the *root* of the trouble lies there. The problem is a human one. The process of learning to love and trust ourselves and live with uncertainty and contradiction may well take most of us a very long time. Those who seem to us to be confident and at ease with themselves may simply be those who are best at keeping themselves and their world under tight control. Those who seem to us uncertain and sometimes thrown off balance may well be those who are confident enough to allow themselves to be shaken. The difficulties of trusting in our own truth and *knowing* what we know most deeply are not peculiar to any one religious group.

Nor am I suggesting that in the Society of Friends all the difficulties belong to those of us who have come from another religious tradition or none at all. I have met and talked with many Friends who have grown up in the Society and felt equally oppressed by the pressures it exerts towards religious conformity. And perhaps none of us is very skilled at the business of answering and respecting that of God in ourselves as well as in others. To be able to do that well, seems to me to require a great deal of sensitivity to what is happening in the depths of our own lives as well as the ability to listen and discern what others are saying to us from the centre of theirs. I do not believe it ever happens without the inward discipline of knowing ourselves and having a compassionate and possibly humourous regard for all that we discover in the process.

I am sure that there are Friends who will want to say that this is all very complicated and that all we need to do is to be obedient to the Spirit and trust God to do the rest. Perhaps it does work like that for some. I happen to believe that wherever the miracle of real communication takes place and people are able to hear and listen to themselves and to one another in a real and deep way that *is* the operation of the Spirit. I have chosen to try and express it differently because I have discovered how easy it is to hide behind religious cliches and jargon and miss the real point of them. The Spirit is the life that flows between and in us all and makes us real to one another. It is only another way of talking about the thing that makes us essentially ourselves. Soul and self and spirit are all metaphors for the same reality.

What makes us bored or dispirited with ourselves and others is when we are still playing a part and not being our real selves, and other people are doing the same. When we have learned the geography of our own hearts and found the treasure within we shall know what George Fox meant when, on the other side of a good deal of painful wrestling with himself and bringing his unknown depths into the light, he was able to say to us 'Go cheerfully over the world, answering that of God in everyone.'[13]

Chapter 9

The Waste Land

The Waste Land, let us say, is any world in which . . . force and not love, indoctrination not education, authority not experience, prevail in the ordering of lives, and where the myths and rites enforced and received are consequently unrelated to the actual inward realisations, needs and potentialities of those upon whom they are impressed.[1]

Joseph Campbell, *The Masks of God*

It is true that the structures of the Church have little to do with the need of the world. That is half the problem. The other half is that they so often have little to do with the need of those within the Church. They do not help us to realise our essential selves — to follow Christ who saves us from being other than who we are. The Church has too often told us what to do and failed to help us become who we can be.[2]

Elizabeth O'Connor, *Inward Journey, Outward Journey*

What are the roots that clutch, what branches grow
Out of this stony rubbish? Son of Man.
You cannot say or guess, for you know only
A heap of broken images, where the sun beats,
And the dead tree gives no shelter . . . [3]

T. S. Eliot, 'The Waste Land'

I have kept my truths: but I have discovered not that they were not truths, but that they were not mine. When I fancied I stood alone I was really in a position of being backed up by all Christendom.[4]

G. K. Chesterton, *Orthodoxy*

From our kitchen window I can see the sharp spire of the Catholic Cathedral. From the summit of the hill its gothic facade, splendidly buttressed and pinnacled, rises to a height of two hundred and eighty feet. It dominates our small town and is a landmark for miles around. From the water meadows of the Arun valley it dominates the skyline as Chartres dominates the great plain of La Beauce. On mornings when I am in a romantic mood it reminds me of Chartres and I can easily imagine that Arundel is a small town in France. It is not in fact remotely like Chartres though it does lend our miniature borough an atmosphere of medieval magic and French charm. On other mornings when I am into self-doubt and despondency (generally when I am suffering from a shortage of sleep or a surfeit of committees) I think it is like me, a pious fraud. At any rate it is not what it seems. One of our Sussex guide books calls it 'pure gothic' which it most certainly is not.

It serves to remind me of how much of my religious life in the past has been a similar (though not entirely fruitless) attempt to imitate medieval models of piety. The flying buttresses on our Cathedral are not functional. They serve no real purpose and offer no real support. They merely decorate the facade of a late nineteenth-century, neo-gothic building which has enough of the spectacular and graceful geometry of a medieval original to confuse the unwary.

Style and spire symbolise a view of Christian belief which belongs to a different time. Medieval Cathedrals were visual primers for illiterate congregations. They taught what the Fathers of the Church judged to be the national curriculum for religious education, with a plentiful display of dire warnings for backsliders and heretics. I suspect that there are not many illiterate Catholics in Arundel today and if there are they are likely to get their visual indoctrination elsewhere. Some of the highly literate Catholics to whom I have talked have read a good deal of contemporary theology, including books by Matthew Fox and Hans Küng and other Catholic writers who are not strictly 'kosher' from the point of view of the Vatican. And at least since Vatican II most of those I know in religious orders are not content to let anyone else do their thinking for them.

But we are not quite into the new age yet and we have no common religious language for speaking about our twentieth-century experiences of God. We do not know whether our pilgrim feet are on new paths or whether, like Chesterton, our excursions into the unknown are simply bringing us by a roundabout route back into orthodoxy. We have to make affirmations of faith which belong to us and to our twentieth-century perceptions of reality or we shall have no way of communicating to others the things that matter most to us. Whether we are, as Eliot suggested, frustrated prophets in a wasted landscape, with only a heap of broken images and a ruined Chapel, empty and open to the wind, I do not know, but for those of us who still find meaning in the Christian myth the wilderness is not, and never can be, God-forsaken. In the Biblical drama it is the desert more often than the temple that is the place of vision.

When I first saw Chartres I was nearly blown out of my mind. I suppose many visitors are. I was overwhelmed, as the faithful were meant to be, by the sheer scale of the place, the brooding atmosphere of mystery, the dignity of those majestic sculptures on the great west portals, the rich mandalas of the Rose windows in the transepts and the dazzling brilliance of multi-coloured glass. I was bound to pay my tribute to the vision and skill of those who had created this vast, mysterious world of glass and stone to mirror their world and make their statement of faith. I was compelled to marvel at what they had done and how they had done it and to envy them the sense of community and the great upsurge of faith which created this awe-inspiring affirmation. It was hard not to feel slightly desolate that with our lost sense of community and our heap of broken images we cannot make that kind of statement. But after an hour or so I began to feel suffocated by the pressure of that world on mine and fled into the sunlight to recover.

In the Spanish Chapel in Florence there is a fresco by Andrea de Firenze. It was commissioned to commemorate the work of the Dominican Order but it also happens to be a vivid symbolic landscape of the medieval world, at least from the point of view of the Church. The background is dominated by a huge church building. The central figures in it are the two Vicars of Christ on earth, the Pope full-centre and the Emperor slightly off-centre. On the right of the Pontiff is an impressive array of ecclesiastic and monastic orders ranked according to the hierarchies of medieval Christendom. On the left of the Emperor a slightly less impressive host of dignitaries and lower social groups represent the secular hierarchies. This may not have been among the Emperor's top ten paintings! At the feet of the two central figures some rather peculiar looking sheep are huddled together guarded, by a pack of fierce-looking dogs. The sheep are the ordinary people, the flock of Christ, over which the Church has assumed absolute control. The dogs are there to guard them from heresy. They are the *Domini Canes*, the dogs of the Lord. It must be hard for contemporary Dominicans to live that one down! The victims of their heresy hunting were likely to be stripped of their legal and political rights as well as their place in the Church. Sometimes their fate was rather worse. In fairness it has to be said that this huge, all-powerful Church provided free social services for the poor, free medical treatment and education for those able to avail themselves of it.

It is not the world in which we live today, though we may marvel at its art and architecture, its sublime statements of faith, its church music, the flowering of its mysticism and the fascinating evolution of its religious orders. European civilisation owes a great deal to the medieval Church and its story is part of us, and can never be lost. No doubt it gave a sense of dignity and reassurance to those whose lives were often nasty, brutish and short, provided you were able to stay within its boundaries, think the right thoughts and keep the rules. But it remains, as Jack Dominian, a Catholic psychiatrist has observed . . . ' A hierarchical system of authority, obedience and sanctions against rule-breakers based on one principle which has had a long history and a wide Christian application: the fear of ultimate rejection in an eternity of hell.'[5]

I have occasionally thought that George Fox was pathological in his reaction to church spires. (Cathedrals produced an even more violent reaction.) 'Their dark power struck at my life.' he wrote again and again in his Journal. When I look at Andrea de Firenze's fresco I can understand his reaction, paranoid though it may have been. Although he was living on this side of the Protestant Reformation he felt that he was still confronted with a Church that was pre-occupied with wealth and status rather than with living out the radical spirituality of the 'Gospel Order.' It still seemed to him to be a Church which wanted power over the lives of human beings rather than one which lived under the authority of the spirit and was concerned about empowering those who belonged to it to discover the sources of life within themselves. He felt oppressed, as I have done, by the shadow side of religious institutions and was right to identify the need to control with the darker side of their corporate life. It seemed to be threatening everything in him that was struggling for life and expression. Something quite vital in him was being done to death by the religious institution in which he had lost himself.

Although the Church has changed, and continues to change, sometimes in response to different social needs or new visions of God and sometimes in order to survive, there is still a massive hangover from the medieval mind-set. It would be comforting to say that it could not happen now, but it does. We do not put people on the rack any more for failing to believe the right things but I still spend a great deal of my time listening to those who feel oppressed or damaged by the religious groups to which they belong or from which they have fled only to find themselves still inwardly crushed by their exposure to religious indoctrination. They have not understood the real nature of the Church's authority and have been so effectively brain washed that they still suffer agonies of guilt either about their departure or their feelings about being oppressed. They feel anxious and ashamed, as well as angry, because they have been unable to extricate themselves emotionally from the pressures to conformity which every religious, and social group exerts.

There are many women today who feel as George Fox

did, that the Church represents a dark power which threatens their creative life. To them its patriarchal structures and hierarchies sometimes seem to have changed very little since Andrea de Firenze painted his fresco which placed them at the bottom or out on the extreme edges of the pyramid of ecclesiastic authority.

Not all of the women to whom I have listened have come from overtly authoritarian Churches. There are those who feel they have been damaged or oppressed within the Society of Friends, as the 1986 Swarthmore Lecture given by the Quaker Women's group made very clear to us. When I spent half a term at Woodbrooke in preparation for the job that I now do I met a woman Friend who had been brought up in a Quaker family, been to a Quaker school and remained in close association with the Society all her life. She regaled me with horror stories about all the events in her Quaker life which had contributed to her very low estimation of herself. One event in particular had lodged in her mind. She had gone back to school with a new velvet dress which was at that point her chief treasure. A prim-lipped matron had taken one look at it and said; 'That is not a suitable dress for a Quaker.' For the rest of her life she wrestled with a sense of shame because of her love of good clothes, rich colours and fine texture. In spite of her later knowledge of Margaret Fox's robust comment 'this is a silly, poor Gospel'[6] when Friends began to pressurise one another into adopting a uniform grey, she was never able to lose the sense of not being a proper Quaker.

Within my lifetime the winds of the spirit have blown at almost hurricane force through the Catholic Church and brought tremendous changes, as well as the inevitable reactionary movements. There are Catholic base communities in Latin America which sound more like Quaker meetings in the way in which vocal ministry has become a shared responsibility. Liberation movements and their expression in new theologies have begun to remind us that the real authority of the Church is one of responsible and loving service and the enabling of the faithful to discover their own power to effect change and their own inner resources for growth and self-direction. These changes have been as incredible as those which have swept through Europe during the time that I was writing this book.

It is much harder I think for the post-Reformation Churches to look more closely at their own structures and become aware in the searching light of the spirit that they did not cease to be authoritarian when they broke away from a system which seemed so oppressive or alien to their understanding of Christian community. I know many within those Churches who have felt equally oppressed by dogmatic views about the authority of the Bible just as I know Quakers who feel oppressed by those who pontificate about what it means to live under the authority of the spirit. There has never been any shortage of authoritarian personalities within any religious group. I have heard Friends asserting, very dogmatically, that—'Quakers are not into sin and guilt' as if awareness that we have somehow missed the mark and grief at the harm we do to ourselves and others were no longer part of the human condition, and often regardless of the fact that another member of their group has just expressed a sense of having made a mess of things.

All Churches today, with the possible exception of a few extremely fundamentalist groups, are facing a crisis in their understanding of the necessary balance between authority and freedom and the tension between personal experience and the corporate expression of religious identity. Friends are wrestling with this too, as our troubled sessions at Aberdeen Yearly Meeting demonstrated. Whenever we meet together to test the concern of an individual Friend, or a group of Friends, who feel that the whole Society should be making statements or doing something about some particular area of social need we have to wrestle with this. And we have our share of Friends who would like to impose their point of view on everyone else. Another of my illusions when I became a member of the Society was that we were a group of human beings who were mature enough to deal with the risks and peculiar anxieties of religious freedom and could cope with the insecurity of making choices without reference to external authorities. Eight and a half years of being what some Friends would call a Quaker bureaucrat have helped to dispel that illusion. I do not know why I was naive enough to imagine that Friends would be free of dependency or the universal symptoms of paranoia. When I began to travel among Friends I found that there were Quaker Universalists who felt that they were not accepted in their Meeting and were somehow made to feel outsiders, and in the same Meeting I would find myself listening to Christo-centric Friends who felt exactly the same. Sometimes their mild paranoia was justified because each group was putting considerable pressure on the other to urge them to conform or drawing mental boundaries which put the other outside. In the beginning of my period of service in Friends House I felt that I was an outsider who would never belong and that those who had been in the Society all their lives and had household names and Quaker pedigrees going back to the seventeenth century were the real insiders. To my amazement I discovered that they often felt as I did or were suffering a much more depressing kind of internal harrassment because they could never live up to their illustrious ancestors.

In fact Friends have particular difficulties with the tension between authority and freedom, and they have had it from the beginning of their history as a dissident religious group. They owe their emergence as a recognisable movement away from the mainstream Christian tradition, to a group of individuals, (and one man in particular), who had discovered in their own experience that it is possible to discover the source of life within yourself, to find God within rather than out there, and to wait in silent attentiveness for the inward promptings of the spirit. It was not, of course, a new discovery. Christians in every Church and those in other religious traditions have made the same discovery whenever circumstance or hunger for more reality in their religious life have compelled them to dig deeper or to open their lives to God in a new way. Other religious groups in the sixteenth and seventeenth centuries were making similar discoveries.

When people fall in love it is so overwhelming an experience that often they cannot believe that anything like it has ever happened to anyone else. They become quite boring or amusing about it. The same kind of thing can happen when people fall in love with God, or make a new discovery about the life of faith. It seems so fresh and startling to them that they cannot believe it has ever happened to anyone else before. It was a bit like that for early Friends and there are still some who think there is such a thing as the Quaker discovery of God!

Perhaps every religious group begins in much the same way with the dynamic experience of one human being who communicates his or her tremendous personal discovery, of what is eternally true, in a fresh way which makes creative use of old and new insights. But for some the new wine bursts the old skin completely and they are compelled, either by exclusion from the main tradition or by voluntary abdication, to make a fresh start. Others who have made similar discoveries somehow manage to stay within the old structure to be both faithful and subversive; or to be suppressed by the mainstream and sometimes to emerge, like Julian of Norwich, speaking with authority to a new age which is ready to receive what once fell on deaf or frightened ears. I am neither a Quaker historian, an ecclesiologist, or a sociologist and can only speak out of my non-expert reading of the situation. Remaining within a particular religious tradition which has become a waste land or no longer reflects your own vision of religious reality or leaving it to become part of something new involve different kinds of loss and adjustment but each is painful.

The history of our Quaker beginnings (apart from records burned in the great fire of London) has been so well documented that we can actually see the way in which early Friends struggled to resolve the problems of authority and religious freedom and how they were eventually compelled to deal with spiritual anarchy and the excesses of individualism by creating their own miniature versions of canon law and a structure of authority which gave Quaker Ministers, Clerks, Elders, and eventually Overseers, functions which regulated and balanced the earlier emphasis on the authority of personal experience. But Friends have never quite recovered from the shock of moving away from what seemed so profoundly new, to become, in certain ways, much more like the institutions against which they had revolted. We still retain some of the flavour of George Fox's adolescent rebellion and seem at times to live with a permanent and extreme aversion to any kind of authority other than what we believe, individually, to be the leading of the spirit.

It is not part of my purpose at this point to focus on the particular changes in society which have led to this new moment of crisis in the Church. Living in a pluralist society in a post-Newtonian age and confronted daily with the evidence of what our lack of awareness has done to the planet on which we live we are bound to wrestle with both the problems of our own complicity in violence and the relativity of all our belief systems. The media reminds us of the horror of totalitarian regimes and of the liberation movements of all kinds which have sprung up in protest against repression. And where the Church is concerned the implications are clear and involve wrestling with what kind of authority it has, if any, to speak prophetically to those who perpetuate unjust systems and also what it must do about those who have been marginalised by its own power structures. The Women's movement, our response to homosexual members, sharpened by the propaganda which accompanied the first public announcements about the spread of the HIV virus, are all salutary reminders to us that oppression and intimidation are not only located in conveniently distant places like South Africa or Latin America.

Whenever I look again at Andrea de Firenze's fresco I find myself wondering how much the Church has changed. I still read books by thoughtful and caring pastors and writers on religious issues who cannot believe that small groups of human beings can be trusted to minister the daily sacraments of forgiveness, healing, encouragement and hope to one another. Some of the books are written by women. They cannot envisage a new age of the spirit in which these things could and should happen. I meet

Quakers, who, after all, have chosen to call themselves a Society of *Friends* who find it hard to trust their own system and rely too much on staff in Friends House or use *Church Government* as a kind of canon law. And yet every day I meet other human beings, sometimes associated with a religious group and sometimes not, who dispense God's grace to me and become *Angels of Annunciation* with a message that seems to be what I need to hear, or *Ministers of Consolation* who do not depart without blessing me.

*　　*　　*

I owe a tremendous debt to feminist writers and theologians who have made me aware of the extent to which women have colluded in their own subordination and allowed social expectations and other people, particularly men (but also their mothers) to write the agenda of their lives for them. I owe a lot to those who have made me even more sharply aware of the disreputable male images of God and models of spirituality which I have imported into my religious life and tried to live with. But I am not convinced, as some are, that women can go it alone in trying to create non-hierarchical ways of living and working together. That conviction has grown as I have met with other women and observed how easily women themselves can be oppressive and autocratic. It has also developed out of the experience of trying to work in a hierarchical structure in a more open and co-operative way.

I am a reasonably open person, and as a pastor and teacher I have always found more satisfaction in opening windows and allowing enough air and light in to enable others to do their own learning than in wanting to have a different kind of authority. I thought it would be relatively easy to work informally in a formal situation and simply enable and encourage others to get on with their own area of work. I reckoned without all the unreal and legitimate expectations which are projected onto any authority figure and all the ambivalent feelings that are projected onto a woman who looks like a friendly mother figure and is not! I failed to realise how much trust is necessary for that kind of experiment and I failed to make it clear that I was going to change the parameters and to find out whether all those involved were willing to work in that kind of open situation. I owe an enormous debt of gratitude to my colleagues in the team who bore with me as I wended my way from blunder to blunder and helped to make it work in spite of the blundering. They helped me to see the mistakes without rubbing salt in the wounds and most of all they were honest and open enough themselves to show me where my own unacknowledged bits of autocracy and passivity got in the way. I learned a lot about the real problems of authority and freedom from that experience of working with a small group.

I was fortunate to have a team with enough strength and vision of their own to prevent me from dominating the enterprise with my bright ideas. We were fortunate in having enough tenacity and courage to hold on while we worked through the inevitable process of our disillusionment with each other. I say fortunate, but of course there was more to it than that. In our different ways we supported and prayed for one another, we learned to forgive one another for the ways in which our unfinished personalities bumped and banged into one another. We learned to listen to one another a little better than we did in the beginning when we were all less confident about our different gifts and strengths and rather less aware of our weaknesses. And we managed to get less heavy and earnest about it all and laugh at our own pathologies. I am not a great lover of religious cliches but whenever we reached a point of real communication with one another, when we forgave and learned the grace of acceptance or gave encouragement to one another to carry on, I saw, and still see, the spirit working in us and between us, making all things new.

I was invited once to talk to a group of Christians in a Church which was an ecumenical partnership between members of the United Reform and Methodist traditions. They wanted to know something about the way in which Friends worship and minister to one another and how we organise our Church affairs. The group was interested, puzzled, and full of questions. They found it hard to imagine a situation in which no single person, or team, holds for life, the responsibilities for pastoral oversight, ministry and religious learning. Eventually the Minister of the Church expressed some envy of a religious society in which those responsibilities are shared. He confessed that he often felt overwhelmed with the burden of work, expectations and obligations which his particular role laid up on him. He went on to say that it would be a great relief to him to be able to shed some of them or at least be able to be known as a real human being, still learning himself. He longed to be able to share some of his own difficulties and his own personal burden of weakness and awareness of failure. At this point there was growing unease in the group and one woman said, to the accompaniment of murmurs of agreement from all but one man, 'But we need you to be strong and caring and clear about what you believe. How shall we know if you don't?'

Some of the problems of authority and freedom, of experience and tradition, were focused for me in that small discussion group as they have been every time a wave of hysteria follows the pronouncements of any Bishop who dares to make his less orthodox convictions known. Hysteria is probably the right word for it because it is all back to the womb stuff, a longing to stay in a warm and comfortable place rather than face a hazardous journey into the unknown. The broken images in T. S. Eliot's terrifying picture of the Waste Land were compounded of quite ordinary material, illusions about human beings and their utopian dreams, the fear of freedom and change, the sterility of closing our minds to new possibilities, the frustration of having trusted others to bring us into a brave new world and the inertia which prefers to stay in the deadness we know rather than risk the humiliation of learning our own destitution, and starting all over again. Years later, when he wrote *The Four Quartets,* he had learned what a long journey in self-knowing is involved if we are to make our deserts blossom for us and come home to ourselves and the place of our beginnings.

*　　*　　*

I often wonder nowadays what kind of Christian I am and whether I qualify, or even want to qualify, as a member of the body of Christ, even on as far out a limb of it as the Society of Friends. And when I hear some Christians defining the Church or what they mean by discipleship I know that I neither belong, or want to belong, in the kind of institution they are talking about. They seem to be describing a rather élite kind of holy club to which only certain kind of people can be admitted or one in which the price for admission involves abandoning a search for truth if it runs counter to anything found in the Club Documents.

I am not, as must be obvious, a great lover of holy clubs or spiritual ghettos. I suppose I shall always have problems with them in spite of the fact that I know that they only reflect, in a heavy corporate way, our own inertia and anxieties about change and loss, our fear of all that is mysterious and unknown and our desire to manipulate the world we know rather than risk a new beginning.

The only interpretations of Christian spirituality that have very much meaning for me today are those I have hammered out for myself, those that are being explored by women, and those that are being created by peaceworkers and groups like the Quaker Youth Theatre. What interpretations of the Gospel I still hold on to (apart from the real guts of the Quaker tradition) are best exemplified by Julian of Norwich and Desmond Tutu.

I can identify with Julian because she managed to live in the kind of Church that Andrea de Firenze painted and to articulate the things she knew on the inside of her life which ran counter to its awesome and frightening theologies, and to do so at a time when women were expected to remain silent on these matters. She must have been a very remarkable woman to have dared to go public with her *Revelations of Divine Love* at a time when the Church was packaging the faith in a way that made God sound like a cross between a Mafia King and the Marquess de Sade. Her vignettes of God as *our homely mother* were painted against the dark backcloth of medieval Doom paintings and frescoes of the Dance Macabre.

She understood intuitively what twentieth-century

scientists are beginning to understand about the nature of the universe. She saw in one of her moments of heightened awareness that the whole cosmos is all of a piece, a vast web of inter-connections held in being by creative energy. For her that energy was the dynamic of the Love of God. She knew at the deepest level of her being what we now know intellectually, that whether you study the structure of the stars or the smallest micro-organism imaginable you are looking at the same basic stuff. For her it was something as small as a hazlenut but she understood that it was 'all that is made.' And when she found herself reflecting on its fragility she understood something more about the indestructibility of the basic kernel of energy in her hands 'It lasts and ever shall last, for that God loveth it. And even so hath everything being by the love of God.'[7]

Desmond Tutu has a different kind of basic simplicity but I warm to an archbishop who can dance his faith and has an engaging grin even for his political opponents and can say to them, and mean it, 'God loves you. God loves me.' For me the heart of the Gospel is there and anything less comprehensive is not good news for anybody. Not long ago a Friend wrote to me expressing grave misgivings about a phrase in *Questions and Counsel.* He was uneasy about it because it made the unequivocal statement that every human being is a child of God. He wanted to add a qualifying clause to the effect that you are a child of God IF ... Quakers are not generally known for their theological refinement but at this point the Revision Committee had got it right, there are no qualifying clauses to the Love of God. But many people, including Christians, as Julian of Norwich observed, find that very difficult to believe. No doubt this is partly because, for some people and perhaps more than we realise, their earlier experiences of parental care have been qualified with explicit or implicit messages ... ' I love you *if* you do what I say ... *if* you are good ... *if* you choose the kind of career ... partner ... lifestyle etc of which I approve.' Because our experience of perfect parenting is bound to be nil it is not always easy for us to grasp the reality of unconditional love, even though in the experience of loving our children we actually do know from the inside what it is like to go on and on caring without deviation.

We also know from our experiences of loving that love involves being vulnerable and that being vulnerable means being wounded. To believe that God is vulnerable in that way is also very difficult for some people to believe, including Christians and in spite of the fact that the central symbol of our faith is the broken body of a man who showed us something incredibly important about the vulnerability of love. In an article in *Chrysalis*, the Journal of the Movement for the Ordination of Women, Janet Morley wrote about her experiments in re-writing liturgy. To her surprise she discovered that talking about God as *she* aroused far less anxiety and offence than naming God as vulnerable. When she re-wrote part of a eucharist prayer for Christmas Eve, which seemed an appropriate enough occasion for remembering the power-shedding of God, and produced the lines:

'Holy, holy, holy, Vulnerable God'[8]

she found herself on the end of barrage of protest. And perhaps that is not surprising when in fact the power structures of the Church are not an obvious declaration about being broken, vulnerable or very much prepared for power-shedding. For us as Friends, however much we find ourselves oppressed by our own particular brand of institutionalism and traditionalism, we know that the only kind of authority we have been given is one which, through the inner imperative of the Holy Spirit, makes us responsible for loving the planet on which we live and caring that its resources should be shared with all the rest of its birthright members. We may know that, but, alas, like every other religious institution, we spend a great deal of our time fussing about the proper maintenance of the structures we do have and far too little of it asking how we can work with others to make the waste lands blossom again.

Chapter 10
Waiting in the Dark

In darkness and anxiety
I searched for her continually
treading again the paths of my confusion
Knowing I knew nothing . . .

In darkness and security
She came to me abundantly touching the
speechless and reluctant part of me
needing to know nothing.[1]

Janet Morley, *All Desires Known*

Women of our generation crowd
forward, voices rich with the
sound of rushing wind, wills
bright as tongues of flame.
From our mothers, from our
children, we reclaim the importance
of our knowing, the power
of our waiting.[2]

Quaker Women's Group, *Bringing the Invisible
into the Light.*

And therefore prepare yourself to
remain in this darkness as long as
you can, ever more crying out to
Him whom you love. For if ever
you shall see Him or feel Him
as far as you can here; it
must always be in this cloud
and in this darkness.[3]

The Cloud of Unknowing

*I am travelling in a wilderness without landmarks. The landscape
is bleak and bare. There are dark mountains and dark shadows. The
sky is a vast emptiness. There is nothing to sustain me . . . nothing*

but the inward voice which says 'wait in this place until you know who you are.' I am alone with all the terrifying 'ifs' of the desert and still the voice says 'wait.'

Mystics and poets know about this experience, so do women who have begun to be aware. In her exploration of the way in which women writers describe the spiritual quest, Carol Christ suggests that it has close analogies with the way the dark night of the soul is described in classical spiritual texts. In her analysis, the wilderness experience for women arises from their sense of emptiness as they become aware of 'their position in a world where women's experience is not valued.'[4]

It is a place familiar to pilgrims and depressives and all explorers of inner space, including, of course, people in religious orders. George Fox knew this interior country very well. His journal records some of his quite intense periods of inward darkness and turmoil. But as John Lampen reminds us in his exploration of the spirituality of George Fox, the original editors of Fox, Naylor and later John Woolman, sometimes felt obliged to suppress accounts of the darker and more mysterious aspects of their spiritual journey.

This practice of editing out the dark or strange has encouraged contemporary Friends in a dreadful unreality about the wholeness of our human experience which must include the dark as well as the light, and to a reluctance to deal truthfully with the conflicts and painfulness of coming into real unity with one another and becoming fully aware of our potential. It has deprived us of 'a mature grasp of experience with its heights and depths.'[5] Or rather it would deprive us if we were to accept the edited versions of Quaker journals as the norm for our own spiritual development.

The wilderness experience or the dark journey seem to be an inescapable part of our human development. The myths and folk tales of every race testify to its reality. It belongs to all those experiences of loss and change which compel us to reframe the questions of adolescence 'who am I?' and 'what is my life for?' But we do not find it easy to talk about this bleak, inner landscape. We are afraid to admit, even to ourselves, that we have been there. The central symbol of the Christian way is one which encapsulates the darkest enigmas of human life and begins at the very point where human optimism or belief in progress are exposed for what they are. Jocelyn Burnell observes in the 1989 Swarthmore Lecture 'In our society success, health, wealth and achievement are applauded, to be positive is an important attitude . . . and subjects like failure, pain, disability are not always acknowledged.'[6]

A Zen master would recognise the darkness and emptiness as the ideal place for enlightenment, but Friends are not very comfortable when they find themselves, either individually or corporately, waiting in the dark. I wonder sometimes whether we *are* very good at *waiting,* in spite of the fact that this is a key word in our Quaker spirituality. Instant coffee and credit cards suggests that people need not wait for anything. Provided we don't mind the *erzatz* taste and high interest rates we can shorten the distance between wanting and getting to an infinitesimal pause between desire and satisfaction. Waiting is a 'discipline' and that word is unpopular too.

Friends can get rather irritable with one another if waiting involves being late for lunch or coming back to an issue again and again until we are clear about what we can do, or can bear to live without an answer. Being in the dark is a problem to us because we have tried to sustain ourselves as a religious group on a serious misunderstanding of what George Fox meant when he urged Friends to 'wait in the light.'

In his pastoral letters, to Meetings or individual Friends, he wrote nothing to imply that waiting on God in stillness would automatically provide us with 150 watts of instant inward illumination. On the contrary he urged Friends to wait with whatever measure of light they *did* have, even if it also meant becoming painfully aware of great areas of inner darkness 'Though you see little, and know little, and have little . . . it is the light that discovers all this, and the love of God to you.'[7]

106

We can be grateful to George Fox for stressing the capacity of all human beings to become aware of their potential for knowing the truth from inside their own experience. It was not a new thought. It was simply a creative rediscovery of the work of the Holy Spirit in human lives. It is what Jesus had promised to his friends. I believe that Jesus was trying to give them confidence in their own potential, their inner resources for growth, for greater awareness and empowerment. We know from our own experiences of loss or crisis that those can be times when we find ourselves inwardly reinforced and able to do things we would have thought impossible. With Anglo-Saxon reticence and our passion for understatement, we look back and say 'I don't know how I did it' or 'I didn't know I had it in me.' But we do have it in us, and the real difficulty is getting us to believe in our own potential.

It was very hard indeed for seventeenth-century Christians to believe in their own possibilities. The Church assured them that they were born in sin and that not even faith in the redemptive work of Christ could cure them of a fatal predisposition to depravity. Because it was such a gloomy and dispiriting picture George Fox took pains to encourage Friends to look at the light, rather than the dark, 'to walk in the light,' and to 'wait in the light.' Unfortunately in trying to give hope to people who felt desperate he overworked the metaphor of the light.

'Light' is a very profound symbol for consciousness and inward knowing. It belongs to all religious traditions, and in the Quaker Tradition it is used in a very distinctive way. The stress that Friends have laid on 'walking in the light' and 'waiting in the light' has left those who accept the seventeenth-century Quaker package without question, with a curiously incomplete understanding of the nature of faith.

Although George Fox was wise enough to point out to over-anxious Friends that their awareness of inner darkness was a sure sign that the searching light of the Spirit was operating effectively in them, he left us with an awkward legacy with regard to living with the contradictions in our lives, contradictions which he did not fully resolve in his own. It was a great comfort to me when I discovered that he was occasionally so oppressed and overwhelmed with darkness that he was unable to go in to a meeting for worship. Some versions of his Journal have edited out this evidence that darkness and depression were still part of his life experience, as they are of ours.

*   *   *

It is a very isolating experience to become aware of the waste land in your own life or to wake up in mid-life, as Dante did, to find yourself in a dark wood, 'where the right way was wholly lost and gone.'[8] Painful and isolating it may be, but it is also a very common experience, and some of the isolation could be eased if we did not suffer from such reticence in learning how to share the darkness.

Until quite recently we have been so heavily conditioned to reticence that many religious people went to hell and back without daring to say anything about it. We are still not very good at sharing our darker experiences. Emotional strip-tease is considered very bad taste by many Friends, as well as highly contagious. I can still remember a conversation with Damaris Parker-Rhodes about this. She had wanted, in her Swarthmore Lecture, to share with Friends an experience of wrestling with her own inner darkness. Members of the Swarthmore Lecture Committee at that time (I don't think it would happen now) were worried that this exposure of the shadow side would somehow transmit itself to others like some kind of 'flu epidemic. It was very distressing to her to be bound to silence about an important, and eventually creative learning experience. For two years after it she went through a period of being unable to speak in Friends meetings. I find that hard to believe when I remember her glorious garrulousness but she assured me it was so.

I do not find it hard to believe at another level. As religious people we can be quite cruel and insensitive to those whose openness or difference threatens the *status quo*, or our own fragile defences. I have sometimes told the

Zen story of the Bishop who came to visit the Master. The Master's disciples were horrified to hear him making the observation that religious people are invaribly rather cruel. 'Why did you tell him that?' they asked when the Bishop had gone. The Master replied 'Religious people are cruel because they so often put their principles and religious practice before people.'[9]

I remember another Friend, a very fine woman Overseer, who was asked to open the session of Yearly Meeting Overseers. She brought her insights in counselling and her experience of pastoral care into that session. What she said fell on very deaf ears at that point, though I am sure it opened up a new way of looking at how we care for one another in our meetings. She too suffered as Damaris Parker-Rhodes had done, and eventually left the Society. Her leaving was not the result of not having been heard in that particular meeting, but it was certainly the result of 'not being heard' whenever she tried to speak on later occasions about her awareness of inward darkness and the need for healing.

It is not surprising, therefore, that a natural reticence about sharing our darkness is reinforced by the fear that others, if we really allow them a glimpse of our inner world, will think we are mad or bad, or have lost our faith. When Margaret Heathfield spoke to Quaker Home Service Representative Council about her work in helping families affected by the Clapham rail disaster in 1989, she reminded us that those who have been thrown off balance by the shock of bereavement or injury need to be reassured that being off-balance and in a state of trauma is not a reflection of their spiritual life. As Paul said, 'your real life is hidden with God in Christ.'[10] Being in a dark place can never mean being in a place without God and being driven into the wilderness is an honourable occupation. It is the place in which we are prepared for service as healers of our society.

Friends who think that 'waiting in the light' means neon lighting along all the darker passages of human experience may need to think again. A lot of faith, it seems to me, is about 'waiting in the dark' and it seems to be psychologically necessary for us to encounter the darkness in ourselves before we are able to release the energy we need for creative living. It is also true that the process of discarding inadequate or misleading images of God and mistaken ideas about what God wants us to do will almost certainly involve us, like Abraham, in going out into the unknown in 'the darkness of faith'. The moment when we become aware that old ways of understanding our lives or envisaging God are no longer possible for us and that we must move out in quest of a new country, is a moment when 'a dread and a great darkness'[11] may fall upon us too.

Faith is not, as some religious seekers and Christian preachers have thought, a matter of shining certainties and spiritual consolation, rather the reverse. When I was a young Deaconess, full of enthusiasm about mission and what I thought was evangelism, I believed that I understood a bit about faith. And so I did. I also learned very quickly what it is not. When I became involved, first as a councillor and later as an advisor, in the first Billy Graham crusades in this country I was very shocked at some of the slick sales talk handed out by over-enthusiastic counsellors. They talked like religious insurance brokers offering fully comprehensive cover for every contingency. I found myself wondering how they managed to fit the anguish and deriliction of Jesus into their full protection policies. I saw other counsellors flapping over the pages of the Bible like high class travel agents selling packaged tours of the 'God country' and offering instant sunshine all the way, with never a touch of winter in the believing heart.

Well, it is not like that, as we all know if we are honest. I have never found much in the Bible to suggest that God offers us any kind of immunity from the more painful aspects of being human. The whole business of being faithful seems to guarantee that you are into the business of getting knocked down or out at fairly regular intervals and that a heightened awareness of suffering as well as joy is part of the real package. The dreadful cry of deriliction from the cross still echoes across two thousand years of church history in which we have tried to dodge its implications and present the invitation to pilgrimage in a more glamorous way. It also reminds us as Friends that waiting in the light is only one side of a paradox.

There were some painful moments in the 1989 Yearly Meeting in Aberdeen. In spite of the excitement of being together in a fascinating city, meeting old friends and making new ones, having fun in creative workshops and worshipping together, we seemed to be a bit destitute and unhappy about ourselves. We were in the dark about what to do about religious language and what it means to be a religious society with its roots deep in the Christian tradition. Instead of being amazed and thankful for the colour and richness of our diversity we seemed a bit uneasy about this and there were pressures to reduce it to a safe and grey conformity.

I shall always be grateful to Ruth Fawell for introducing me, in *The Courage to Grow,* to the letters of John Keats and in particular to his use of the term 'negative capability'. In a letter to his brothers in December 1817, he wrote, 'Negative capability is when a man is capable of being in uncertainties, mysteries, doubts, without any irritable reaching after fact and reason.'[12] Ruth Fawell interprets this as a way of making the best use of all our experience, dark as well as light. I would want to add that for me it includes the ability to live without fretting about the contradictions in our own lives, the dark as well as the light of our being, and without becoming too fretful or impatient about the contradictions within the Society of Friends.

Faith is not, and cannot be, only about waiting in the light in the way that we have sometimes understood that phrase. It is certainly not what George Fox meant. His own life included passages of darkness and depression which continued long after his conversion experience. If we lived with blazing certainties and well lit paths through the wilderness we would not need faith at all. It is about living with 'uncertainties, mysteries, and doubts' and with what the mystical tradition calls the *via negativa*. Although we may prefer bright and breezy affirmations of faith there are actually vast tracts of unknowing and inner darkness to be negotiated, and like Dostoevsky, our hallelujahs must often come out of 'the crucible of doubt.'[13]

Chapter 11
Silence, Simplicity and Integration

Silence and love, rooted in the Gospel and a
loving group are the culture in which the seed
of awareness may grow.[1]
Damaris Parker-Rhodes, *Truth — a Path and not a*
Possession

The first Quaker book I read was Thomas Kelly's *Testament of Devotion*. It was during one of the first of our college's Quiet Days. We had a small library of devotional books and spiritual classics which was housed in the college chapel. I found the *Testament* there and carried it away as treasure trove to mull over during the strangeness and luxury of a whole day of silence. It seems oddly appropriate to me now that in those far off days when I was preparing myself for service as a 'Deaconess in the Church of God,' it was a Quaker who first helped me to understand the meaning of 'holy obedience' and simplicity, and taught me how to use silence.

Equally interesting to me now is the fact that it was a Quaker writer who first made me aware that 'self-knowing' is a necessary part of spiritual growth. Thirty years later another Friend introduced me to the ideas of *Psychosynthesis*. He and his wife led a workshop on Assagioli's multi-polar model of human personality. They led us through a series of guided fantasies to the discovery of some of our sub-personalities. I remember that I felt a bit dazed by the motley bunch I found in the rooms in my imagined house. There was a rather zany Don Quixote type, a mad, faceless artist, a youthful poet, an old hermit, a mute Joan of Arc figure, a very small child and a blowsy trollop. I always wondered whether the fact that I had been reading Hesse's *Steppenwolf* a few days before had some effect on the bizarre selection of sub-personalities that my psyche managed to produce.

It was Thomas Kelly, not Assagioli, who first introduced me to the idea of the human being as an assembly of persons. In his chapter on 'the Simplification of Life' he describes us as 'not a single self, but a whole committee of selves . . . And each of our selves is in turn a rank individualist . . . '[2] Real simplicity, in his view, was the process of integrating our different selves by attending to what is being spoken in the deepest centre of our lives. What Thomas Kelly discovered, during the same period as the Italian psychologist Assagioli was presenting his papers on psychosynthesis, has helped me to go on using the Quaker way of becoming centred in silence as one way of listening to and learning how to integrate my many selves. Some of the things that Thomas Kelly wrote about holy obedience and simplicity I would find problematical now, but his insight into the multi-polar aspects of personality is one that I still find valuable.

*　　*　　*

There is one aspect of myself, an austere self, that is very much at home in the stark simplicity of a traditional Quaker meeting house. It may be no more than a mixture of puritan inclination, aesthetic pleasure, emotional need and a dash of religious romanticism. Whatever the mixture there is something in me which responds to the bare room stripped of all holy images and symbols except the potent symbolism of the empty space, the silence and the sense of waiting.

After the emotional upheaval in my life prior to attending my first meeting I was famished for silence. I needed it as desperately as the children I met in Ghana were desperate for food. I needed it to cool my over-heated emotions and as a space to re-order my life. I have found it quite impossible to separate the different strands in the cords that drew me towards the Society of Friends. In the beginning it was theological interest and a feeling of affinity with Quaker Spirituality. Later it became an intellectual need to find a space for God-exploration which was not so hemmed in or blocked by doctrinal hedges or credal *cul-de-sacs*.

In the end it seemed to be an emotional need for inner simplicity which tore down the last of my defences against making a journey that had become almost inevitable. I was aware of so much clutter in my life. Early Friends would call it 'cumber.' My head was always too full of ideas. My emotions were over-heated. My diary was too full of engagements. I was too busy for contemplation, too busy for my friends, too busy to listen to those I cared about, too busy to listen to myself. I had lost touch with something vital in myself. It had taken what Robert Louis Stevenson described as 'a piercing pain, a killing sin'[3] to bring my dead self back to life. Even the times I set aside for prayer and contemplation were breathless with my inner anxiety and my sense of being overwhelmed with obligations. God was somehow among the obligations that were weighing me down.

What did I hope for when I came among Friends? Did I imagine that I would somehow catch inward stillness like an infection, or that I would find the habit of quietness again as I sat with Friends learning a new language for God in the syllables of silence? Was I foolish and naive enough to hope that Quakers, with their wholesome simplicities, would be able to save me from myself? Did I imagine that they were different from the rest of the human race, more tolerant and accepting, able to accept all that I could not bear to acknowledge in myself?

I suppose we all bring some unrealistic expectations with us when we move away from one religious group into another, or become involved in one for the first time. It is not unlike the unrealistic expectations with which we enter into relationships. We find that some of our hopes are realised, not always as we expected. Some of our deepest needs are satisfied, but others are not. And in each case we have to move beyond our illusions to learn the difficult art of acceptance, which is almost impossible until we have learned to accept ourselves.

At first I thought that Quaker simplicity was all a matter of theological convincement and style. Friends were into simplicity because it was the inevitable outcome of believing certain things about God and human beings. If you really cared about the truth you were into plain language. If

you cared about equality or the poor you were into plain
dress, and a simple lifestyle. If you cared about real religion
you were into unadorned meeting houses and no religious
bric-a-brac. It all seemed to hang together as a part of what
George Fox called the 'Gospel order'. Since then I have discovered how simplistic, rather than simple, my thinking
was, and how many illusions I carried with me when I
crossed the threshold of a Quaker meeting house.

One of the first I attended was at Long Sutton in Somerset. We were staying with some old friends in the village of
Curry Mallet. One of them had recently joined the Society.
We went with them to Long Sutton on a drowsy summer
morning. Bees hummed in the old flower filled garden.
Sunlight fell on the graceful simplicity of a Queen Anne-
style meeting house and on the plain, unadorned grave-
stones. It was all rather idyllic. I knew nothing at the time
about the history of the Long Sutton meeting, punctuated
with periods of persecution and harassment which would
have shattered any notion that being a Friend involves
having a peaceful life. I did not know then that there had
been a regular meeting for worship in that village since
1668. All I knew, as we sat on hard benches in the cool stillness of the 18th century meeting room with its plain, unvar-
nished wood and smooth flagstones, was that I felt a sense
of peace and rightness in being there.

Long Sutton Meeting was idyllic on that sun-filled day in
late August. It fed my illusions about Quaker silence and
simplicity. It was austere. It was full of a rich stillness, hall-
owed with memories of George Fox and his meeting with
the Somerset Seekers in 1656, soon after his release from
Launceston Gaol. I did not know the story then. I did know
that the meeting house had about it that air of awesome and
powerful stillness that I have sometimes felt in the quiet
corners of the cloisters of a great cathedral. It is almost as if
the stone walls and ancient wood have absorbed into themselves the memory of earlier pilgrims and created from their
lives a field of energy.

Mike Harding, the travel writer and comedian, felt it too,
when he visited Brigflatts meeting house and tried to

describe the special quality of stillness that surrounds and infuses it. He suggests that if we can accept scientifically that stone in the form of silicone chips can accept and retain messages, we should not be surprised if old stones retain a memory of powerful emotions imprinted on them in earlier times, fear or faith, terror or trust, prayer and worship. Long Sutton made that kind of impression on me—'a peaceful house, in a peaceful place'.[4] It had a quality of stillness which, at the time, seemed very far removed from the hassle and rush of my life, teaching deprived and maladjusted children in Cardiff, preaching in Welsh chapels, helping to run house groups, and a home, as well as training voluntary counsellors for work in a branch of the Westminster Pastoral Foundation.

* * *

Fortunately the first Meeting where I became a regular Attender was quite different from Long Sutton. It demolished some of my illusions quite quickly. It was held in a shabby, solid, three-storey Victorian house in a rather down-at-heel road just off the main shopping centre in Cardiff, and next door to a Night Club. Marks and Spencers was at one end of the road. The other end was in a state of demolition and re-building for most of the time we were there. We worshipped to the sound of bulldozers and falling masonry. I learned very quickly that inward stillness has nothing to do with the sound of bees and bird-song in a country garden.

A few weeks before I began to attend Cardiff meeting I had been on holiday with some friends in Cardiganshire. I remember one very hot day when we walked for miles along a coastal path. It was very wild and remote. The cliffs were covered with late summer flowers. The occasional Shag or Cormorant flew past but we met no other walkers as we tramped northwards. Eventually the path dipped downwards towards the sea and ran beside a small natural pool about thirty feet across and almost cut off from the incoming tide by a circular wall of huge rocks. We were very hot and tired. Two of us stripped and let ourselves down into the cool, dark water. The pool was very deep. Not once did we touch or catch sight of the bottom. We swam, floated, trod water and eventually scrambled out feeling marvellously refreshed and invigorated.

My first meeting for worship has always reminded me of that experience. I had left one way of life behind, weary with trying to make sense of it and with trying to fit myself into it. I walked into a meeting where I knew no one. Silence was not strange to me, but Quaker worship was. I felt as if I were stripping my spiritual life down to the bare essentials and letting myself down into something which was both strange and familiar. I knew that I was out of my depth. I still am, and thank God, always will be. But I found the silence cool and refreshing.

Thomas Kelly writes about the 'Divine Abyss'[5] in each of us, a term which makes me think, irreverently, of black-robed Mother Superiors rather than bottomless depths. But I know what he meant. Quaker spirituality is about letting ourselves down into a deep place. It involves us in living from the deepest centre of ourselves where the real prayers of our life are made and learning to trust our inward knowing. It is about daring to believe in the reservoir of power and wisdom which is available to us when we stop trying to control the world and surrender ourselves to a process of inward direction.

Jesus put it another way when he spent his lunch hour talking to a Samaritan woman about her thirst for reality. She was not the kind of woman you might expect to be very fervent about real religion. He was not the kind of man she expected to pay much attention to someone of her race and gender. They both forgot and found themselves in a moment of real meeting when he was eager to tell her what he had learned in his own life, that she must learn to trust her inner resources, the holy centre in herself. Like many women she found it hard to believe in herself, to trust her own insights or to know herself gifted by God. Others had always defined her life for her, chiefly men. It was strange to her to be urged by one of them to ignore what others had told her and learn to trust the source of life springing up at the centre of herself.

I get huge enjoyment from the thought that Quaker worship was justified by George Fox on the basis of this lunchtime conversation between two outsiders. It is to this slightly disreputable woman that Jesus is reported to have spoken about the end of formal religion and the beginning of a new age of the Spirit in which real prayer and worship will be understood in terms of what really goes on inside people at the deepest places in their lives, 'in spirit and in truth.' I am sure it was not merely incidental that Jesus was more at ease talking to a woman with a certain wayward lust for life than to the religious leaders of his day who had an urge to control it.

It is not religion that matters so much. It is life. It is not religion that requires our deepest respect and reverence. It is life, the life springing up in ourselves and others, the life of all living things and of the planet on which we pursue our inter-connected lives. Real religion is always liberating and helps us to be aware of the holy thing that Life is. Its purpose is to make us more, rather than less, alive, and to free us from whatever restricts the flow of life within us. Irenaeus, the first great Catholic theologian, protested vigorously against the kind of spirituality which negated the incarnation. He insisted that if Christians really believed that they had seen the embodiment of God in a human being it meant that human nature and the material world were to be treasured and celebrated. God was not to be found by denying the richness of human life and experience but by entering more deeply into them. 'The glory of God' wrote Irenaeus, 'is a human being fully alive.'[6]

At its richest Quaker spirituality is a testimony to the goodness of creation and the sacramental nature of the whole of Life. It belongs, as the Dominican, Matthew Fox reminds us, to the tradition of 'creation-centred' spirituality and celebrates both the glory and blessing of the world we can see and the treasure of our hidden potential. At its best it represents a refusal to run away from the problems of being human and an engagement with life which involves us in wrestling to bring to an end all that is oppressive and diminishing. At its worst it can be as dualistic and life-denying as the worst of medieval Christianity, Puritanism and Victorian churchianity put together. Perhaps there is never more than a razor edge between real religion and the kind that encourages us to look for escape routes, insurance policies and fortresses.

The razor's edge is part of my experience too. No doubt it will remain so for the rest of my life, or at least until I can achieve real simplicity which is only another way of talking about integration or wholeness. When I first became part of the Quaker community I thought that simplicity was all about getting rid of 'cumber' and stripping down my life to a few things that really mattered. I was more interested in austerity than in learning to love the world in my heart. Now I begin to see that it may be much more to do with a wholehearted and joyful acceptance of all that I am and a willingness to allow my many selves to be integrated by obedience to the inner law of my own being. Some Friends will want to name that inner law as God, or Truth or Inward Light. Others may be happy to call it Spirit or their real and deepest self, their divine centre. I am not sure that the labels are as important as we sometimes think.

I remember a moment in my life when I was tempted to jettison everything that I knew of truth and integrity for the sake of something more immediately gratifying. The victories of love are always a bit ambiguous. At the time it felt as if I was saying 'no' to a real chunk of life. In the process of doing so I felt as if I was dying. But I knew that in that moment of saying 'no' I was actually saying 'yes' to something much more important, something deep within me which claimed my total allegiance. It does not seem to me to matter very much whether I label that inward imperative as God or Holy Spirit, as truth or love or the inward law of my being. I know that I was addressed by an inward voice more imperative than the clamouring voices of my many selves.

It was at that moment of inward surrender that I knew I must find my way to the Society of Friends. I knew in my own experience, consciously and unequivocally, what Thomas Kelly meant when he talked about real simplicity as surrender to this 'holy thing within us'.[7] I did not know it then as a continuous process of inward listening and enlightenment. There are still plenty of times when my unruly committee of selves say to one another, as Oscar Wilde is reported to have said to his friend, Robbie, about the Last Trump, 'Let's pretend we don't hear it.' But I felt that the time had come for me to throw in my lot with those who practice the art of inward listening in their worship and life.

It is in the silence of Quaker worship, in learning to listen more deeply to myself or to what Thomas Kelly calls the 'divine centre, the holy thing within us',[7] and also in journal writing, in meditation on crowded commuter trains and in self-awareness exercises that I have made some surprising discoveries. They may not surprise those who have travelled much further than I have in the exploration of inner space. I have discovered, for example, that the puritan in me, which I had thought of as moral and good, is actually the part of me that is most afraid of life. It is the part of me that wants to be in control, approves of an ordered and disciplined life and colludes with formal religion and education in attempting to suppress the unknown and uncontainable creative energies within me. It is the self that purses its lips in disapproval when the holy child in me wants to play or dance.

More recently feminist theologians and the Quaker Women's group have made me more aware of the 'oppressed woman' in my committee of selves. For a long time I failed to recognise her at all. I was naive enought to think that having responsible jobs, plenty of scope for my initiative and skills and some considerable zest in fighting my own corner meant that I was liberated. I was fortunate in having male colleagues who were generally considerate (much more than I was!) and sensitive. I enjoyed working with them and learned a lot from them. I was still blissfully unaware that my stubborn and aggressive determination to be heard was itself evidence of the real situation. It did not dawn on me for some time that my spiritual progress (or regress) into dissidence and heresy was largely a protest against the patriarchy I had never really questioned except in terms of its deviance from the New Age Community apparently envisaged by Jesus. It never occurred to me that my reaction was often, though not always, more like adolescent rebellion than real freedom. It has taken me a long time to trust the holy woman in myself and her hidden wisdom without needing to be fierce or pugnacious about it.

Looking back I recognise that it was more than a need to re-organise my life and simplify it which led me to choose silence. I needed the silence as an outward expression of an inner journey away from male images as metaphors for the Holy. I would not have known how to put it in words at the time but an inward prompting was pushing me further into the unknown. Finding the Holy in myself has meant leaving behind a lot of ways of picturing God which have been important to me in the past. No doubt we all have to make such journeys sooner or later in order to discover what is real for us and to become a bit more grown up spiritually. I seem to have taken a very long time to understand what the five year old daughter of a colleague of mine understood when she said: 'the God in me is a she.' And it has taken me nearly as long to understand that the God with whom we have to do wants us to grow up and stand on our own feet even if the community of faith to which we belong is uneasy about our spiritual independence.

God is the symbolic language we have used to express what seems to be most profound and mysterious in our lives, the ultimate Reality or, as Tillich described it, 'the ground of our being'.[8] Our deepest human experiences may tell us more about the Reality than all the books that have been written to try and express the mysterious familiarity and otherness of God and the ways in which the seeds of new life are nourished in our lives. But no human metaphors or models will ever be able to contain it. We may invent new names to help us to explore the mystery. We may select the ones which seem to bring us closest to God and think of her or him as our Lover, our dependable Friend, our neighbour God or the mysterious process of energy and exchange through which the universe evolves, but in the end we cannot domesticate God. In the silence of Quaker worship I have sensed the seed of life growing within me and in the still centre where that life unfolds I can dispense with all the metaphors and models which have helped and hindered me. The language of my heart is not exclusive and in the vast syntax of silence, when the grammar of love has become my first and second language, I shall know the world within me as I am known and come home to myself with my own *Nunc Dimmitis* and *Glorias*.

Or perhaps I shall not need any words at all.

References

1 George Fox, 'The Pearl Found in England', *Gospel Truth Demonstrated in A Collection of Doctrinal Books*. Vol I (first printed 1706). Reprint of 1831 edition, AMS Press, 1975, p. 164.

2 Adrienne Rich, 'Natural Resources', in *The Dream of a Common Language*. W & W Norton, 1978, p. 64.

3 Gerard Manley Hopkins, 'As Kingfishers Catch Fire', in *Selected Poems*. Heinemann, 1953, p. 52.

CHAPTER 1—Turning Point

1 Matthew Fox, *On Becoming a Musical, Mystical Bear*. Paulist Press, 1972, Preface, p. x.

2 Esther de Waal, *Living With Contradiction*. Collins: Fount Paperbacks, 1989, p. 40.

3 Melvyn Matthews, *The Hidden Journey*. Collins: Fount Paperbacks, 1989, p. 40.

4 Rudolph Otto, *The Idea of the Holy*, translated by John Harvey. Oxford University Press, 1958.

5 Stevie Smith, 'The Galloping Cat' in *The Collected Poems of Stevie Smith*. Penguin, 1985, p. 563.

6 Gerald Priestland, *Something Understood*. Arrow Books, 1988. p. 248.

7 Martin Buber, *The Way of Response*. Selections from his Writings, edited by N N Gatzer. Schocken Books, 1966, p. 41.

8 Meister Eckhart, sermon: 'Qui Audit Me', quoted by Don Cupitt and used as the title for *Taking Leave of God*. SCM Press, 1980.

9 Lao Tsu, *Tao te Ching*. Translated Gia-Fu Feng & Jane English. Wildwood House, 1973, No. 56.

10 *Acts* 17:28, *Revised Standard Version*.

CHAPTER 2—Year of Jubilee

1 T S Eliot, 'Little Gidding' in *Four Quartets*. Faber & Faber, 1959, p. 55.

2 Kallistos Ware, *The Orthodox Way*. Mowbrays, 1979, p. 36.

3 T S Eliot, 'East Coker' in *Four Quartets*. Faber & Faber, 1959, p. 31.

4 William Littleboy in *Christian Faith & Practice*. London Yearly Meeting, 1960, §81.

5 W H Auden, 'The Summons' from 'For the Time Being' in *Collected Longer Poems*. Faber & Faber, 1974, p. 159.

6 *Methodist Hymn Book*. Methodist Conference Office, 1933, No: 608.

7 J Neville Ward, *Beyond Tomorrow*. Epworth Press, 1981, p. 1.

CHAPTER 3—Knowing Experimentally

1 Kenneth Clark, *Moments of Vision*. John Murray, 1981, p. 16.

2 George Fox, *Journal*, ed. by J L Nickalls, London Yearly Meeting, 1952, rptd. 1975, p. 27. Entry for 1648.

3 *Luke* 18 v 17. *New Jerusalem Bible*. Doubleday, 1985.

4 George Fox, *Journal*, ed. by J L Nickalls. London Yearly Meeting, 1952, p. 19. Entry for 1647.

5 Margaret Fell in *Christian Faith & Practice*. London Yearly Meeting, 1960, §20.

6 Douglas Steere, (Ed) *Quaker Spirituality, Selected Writings*. SPCK, 1984. Introduction, p. 15.

7 Martin Israel, 'The Path to Life' in *Precarious Living*. Mowbray, 1976, p. 16.

8 Kenneth Boulding, *There is a Spirit*, the Naylor Sonnets. Fellowship Publications, 1979, p. 1.

9 Edwin Muir, 'One Foot in Eden' in *Collected Poems*. Faber & Faber, 1960, p. 227.

10 Gerard Manley Hopkins, 'God's Grandeur' in *Selected Poems*. Heinemann, 1953, p. 18.

CHAPTER 4—In and Out of Time

1 Kallistos Ware, *The Orthodox Way*. Mowbray, 1979, p. 25.

2 Rainer Maria Rilke. Letters to a Friend. Untraced.

3 Shunryu Suzuki, *Zen Mind, Beginner's Mind*, ed. by Tracy Dixon. Weatherhill, 1970, rptd. 1982, p. 21.

4 *Psalm* 119:71.

5 Maud Monahan, *Life and Letters of Janet Erskine Stuart*. Longmans, 1953, p. 75.

CHAPTER 5—My Own Woman

1 'I Danced' in *I Hope So*. Poetry by Quaker Womens Group, 1988, p. 4.
2 Hadewijch of Brabent, 'The Power of Love', in *Beguine Spirituality*, ed. by Fiona Bowie, trans. by Oliver Davies. SPCK, 1989, p. 124.
3 George Herbert, 'Prayer', in *Oxford Book of Christian Verse*. Chosen and edited by Lord David Cecil. Oxford University Press, 1941, No: 106, p. 139.
4 J H Oldham, *Life is Commitment*. SCM Press, 1953, p. 79.

CHAPTER 6—Moments of Awareness

1 Edith Sitwell, 'How Many Heavens', in *Collected Poems*. Macmillan, 1982, p. 306.
2 Melvyn Matthews, *The Hidden Journey*. Collins: Fount Paperbacks, 1989, p. 147.
3 Kathleen Raine, 'Message from Home', in *Collected Poems*. Hamish Hamilton, 1963.
4 George Fox, *Journal*, ed. by J L Nickalls. London Yearly Meeting, 1952, rptd. 1975, p. 27. Entry for 1648.
5 *Ibid*, p. 46-47. Entry for 1649.
6 1 *Peter* 4:10 (my paraphrase)
7 C S Lewis, 'The Day with a White Mark' in *The Poems of C S Lewis*, ed. by Walter Hooper. Bles, 1964, p. 28.
8 *Psalm* 118:24.

CHAPTER 7—Heart Work

1 Rainer Maria Rilke, 'Turning', quoted by Elizabeth Watson in *'Guests of my Life'*, Celo Press, 1983, p. 72, from *Letters of Rainer Maria Rilke*, Vol. 2—1910-1926. Translated by Jane Barnard Greene and M. D. Herter Norton. N. W. Norton, 1947, rptd. 1948. An alternative translation is found in Rainer Maria Rilke, *Poems 1906-26*. Translated by J. B. Leishman. Hogarth Press, 1957, rptd. 1976, p. 184.
2 Damaris Parker Rhodes. *Truth—a Path and not a Pos-*

REFERENCES

session. Swarthmore Lecture, 1977. Friends Home Service Committee, 1977, p. 67.

3 John Drury, *The Burning Bush*. Collins: Fount Paperbacks, 1990, p. 20.

4 Julian of Norwich, *Revelations of Divine Love*. The Thirteenth Revelation. Chapter XXVII, pp. 55-57. Edited by Grace Warrack. Methuen, 1901, rptd. 1917.

5 1 *John*, 3:2. *Authorised Version*.

6 *Matthew*, 16:26 (my paraphrase).

7 Thomas Merton. Untraced.

CHAPTER 8—Spirituality as Awareness

1 Julian of Norwich. *Revelations of Divine Love*. Ed. Grace Warrack. Methuen, 1901, rptd. 1917. Chapter LVI, p. 135.

2 Lionel Blue, *Bolts from the Blue*. Hodder and Stoughton, 1986, p. 137.

3 Damaris Parker Rhodes, *Truth—a Path and not a Possession*. Swarthmore Lecture, 1977. Friends Home Service Committee, 1977, p. 57.

4 Anthony de Mello, S. J., *One minute Wisdom*. Anand Press, 1985, p. 10.

5 Meister Eckhart. Untraced.

6 *The Gospel of St Thomas*. I have been unable to trace the translation in my common place book. Variant translations can be found in Hugh McGregor Ross, *The Gospel of Thomas*. Ebor Press, 1987, pp. 50, 70 and 83.

7 William Penn's Preface to George Fox's *Journal*. Ed. J. L. Nickalls. London Yearly Meeting, 1952, rptd. 1975, p. xiii.

8 Douglas Steere, 'On being Present Where You Are', in *Together in Solitude*. Crossroad Publishing, 1982, p. 158.

9 Jean Pierre de Caussade, *Self-Abandonment to Divine Providence*. Counsel 2. Translated by Algar Thorold. Edited by Father John Joyce. S. J. Burns and Oats, 1959, p. 5.

10 Carl Gustav Jung, *Modern Man in Search of a Soul*. Routledge and Kegan Paul, 1961, pp. 271-2.

11 Damaris Parker Rhodes, *The Way Out is the Way In*. Quaker Home Service, 1985, p. 177.
12 Rainer Maria Rilke, *Later Poems*, translated by J. B. Leishman. Hogarth Press, 1938. A variant translation is found in *Poems 1906-26* translated by J. B. Leishman, Hogarth Press, 1976, p. 193. I am indebted to Elizabeth Watson for introducing me to Rilke's poems in *Guests of My Life*. Celo Press, 1983.
13 George Fox, in *Christian Faith and Practice*. London Yearly Meeting, 1960, §376.

CHAPTER 9—The Waste Land

1 Joseph Campbell, *The Masks of God*, Vol. IV. *Creative Mythology*. Penguin, 1968, p. 388.
2 Elizabeth O. Connor, *Inward Journey, Outward Journey*. Harper & Row, 1968, p. 32.
3 T S Eliot, 'The Waste Land'. *Selected Poems*. Faber & Faber, 1958, p. 51.
4 Gilbert Keith Chesterton, *Orthodoxy*. Fontana, 1961, p. 12.
5 Jack Dominion, *Authority*. Darton, Longman and Todd, 1981, p. 3.
6 Margaret Fox, in *Christian Faith and Practice*. London Yearly Meeting, 1960, §401.
7 Julian of Norwich, *Revelations of Divine Love*. Translated by James Walsh, S. J. Anthony Clarke, 1980, p. 53.
8 Janet Morley. 'Wordwatch', *Chrysalis* (Movement for the Ordination of Women), July 1989.

CHAPTER 10—Waiting in the Dark

1 Janet Morley. 'In darkness and anxiety', in *All Desires Known*. Movement for the Ordination of Women, 1988, p. 55.
2 Quaker Women's Group. *Bringing the Invisible into the Light*. Swarthmore Lecture, 1986. Quaker Home Service, 1986, p. 96.
3 Anon. *The Cloud of Unknowing*. Translated by Robert Way. Anthony Clarke, 1986, p. 12.

REFERENCES

4 Carol Christ, *Diving Deep and Surfacing*. Beacon Press, 1980, p. 14.
5 John Lampen, *Wait in the Light*. Quaker Home Service, 1981, p. 71.
6 Jocelyn Burnell, *Broken for Life*. Swarthmore Lecture, 1989. Quaker Home Service, 1989, p. 1.
7 Cecil Sharman, *No more but my love*. Letters of George Fox. Quaker Home Service, 1980. Letter 9, p. 8.
8 Dante Alighieri, *The Divine Comedy*, 1: Hell. Translated by Dorothy L. Sayers. Penguin, 1949, p. 71.
9 Anthony de Mello, S. J. *One Minute Wisdom*. Anand Press, 1985, p. 107 (adapted).
10 *Colossians 3:3. Revised Standard Version.*
11 *Genesis 15:12 Revised Standard Version.*
12 John Keats in a letter to his brothers dated 21 December 1817 in *The Life and Letters of John Keats*. Dent: Everyman's Library, 1927, p. 62.
13 Feodor Dostoevsky. Untraced.

CHAPTER 11 — Silence, Simplicity and Integration

1 Damaris Parker Rhodes. *Truth — a Path not a Possession*. Swathmore Lecture, 1977. Friends Home Service Committee, 1977, p. 35.
2 Thomas Kelly, *Testament of Devotion*. Hodder and Stoughton, 1957, p. 105.
3 Robert Louis Stevenson, *Poems*. Chatto and Windus, 1914, p. 31.
4 Mike Harding, *Walking the Dales*. Michael Joseph, 1986, p. 103.
5 Thomas Kelly, *Testament of Devotion*. Hodder and Stoughton, 1957, p. 105.
6 St Irenaeus. 2nd century. Quoted in *Fully Human, Fully Alive*. John Powell, S. J. Argus, 1976, p. 7.
7 Thomas Kelly, *Testament of Devotion*. Hodder and Stoughton, 1957, p. 107.
8 Paul Tillich, *The Shaking of the Foundations*. Pelican, 1962, p. 62.